MADNESS AND CREATIVITY

Madness and Creativity

Peter J. Buckley

IPBOOKS.net
International Psychoanalytic Books

International Psychoanalytic Books (IPBooks)
New York • http://www.IPBooks.net

Madness and Creativity

Published by IPBooks, Queens, NY
Online at: www.IPBooks.net

ISBN: 978-1-956864-02-1

For Eric and Jo
Who Inspired Me

ACKNOWLEDGMENTS

THANKS to Maxine Antell, Helene Eisenberg, Robert Freedman, Philip Herschenfeld, Margaret Hornick, Tobias Kampf, Salvatore Lomonaco, Ronnie Scharfman, and Linda Schrank.

TABLE OF CONTENTS

∞

"There really is no such thing as Art. There are only artists."
–E.H. Gombrich
"Melancholy is my joy and discomfort my rest."
–Michelangelo

INTRODUCTION

❧

The putative relationship between mental illness and creativity is of long-standing cultural and psychological interest.

The legend of the great artist as 'possessed' dates back to antiquity and Plato's articulation of 'divine madness'. The underlying fantasy, I would suggest, revolves around the popular belief that original and ground-breaking art is inspired by other-worldly forces outside the realm of quotidian experience. As an anonymous traveler commented on entering Giotto's *Arena Chapel* (painted in Padua, Italy, 1350): "I have arrived in Paradise."

The psychological impact of encountering great works of art, distinct from the conventional esthetic experience, can be dramatic and reinforce this sense of 'divine' origins.

The French novelist Stendhal described the effect on his psyche of the paintings, tombs and sculpture in the Renaissance Florentine church of *Santa Croce*: "My emotion is so profound that it verges on piety. The gloomy religiousness of this church, its simple wood ceiling, its unfinished façade, everything talked vividly to my soul.... I was already in a sort of ecstasy... Leaving Santa Croce, my head pulsed... the life in me was exhausted: I walked in a fear of falling." (1)

At issue, and central to his book, are the psychological elements that enhance and catalyze creativity. Is mental illness in the artist a factor? The evidence is mixed. That certain great artists have, at times, been clinically 'mad' is indisputable. The composer Robert Schumann, the painters Vincent van Gogh and Edvard Munch, the novelists Virginia Woolf and David Foster Wallace are notable examples. Whether their serious episodic psychiatric illnesses contributed to, or were inimical to, their creative work, remains a question.

The complex nature of creativity is central to this dispute. Some have suggested that the truly creative person has a capacity for psychological 'regression' that can plumb the darker regions of the unconscious and then utilize these experiences, now under the sway of the rational ego, to produce original great art. (2) Hieronymus Bosch and Goya with their startling phantasmagoric imagery would be examples.

This capacity is not necessarily a manifestation of mental illness *per se*, but may be a reflection of an innate capacity for an inner psychological journey that enables the artist to tap the normally unseen and then express it.

Nancy Andreasen's seminal study, *Creativity and mental illness: Prevalence rates in writers and their first-degree relatives*, examined the rates of mental illness in 30 creative writers, 30 matched control subjects, and the first-degree relatives of both groups. She discovered that the writers had a substantially higher rate of mental illness, predominantly affective disorder, with a tendency toward the bipolar subtype. She also found that there was a higher prevalence of affective disorder and creativity in the writer's first-degree relatives, suggesting that these traits ran together in families and could be genetically mediated. Further, both writers and controls had IQs in the superior range: the writers excelled only on the WAIS vocabulary subset, suggesting that intelligence and creativity are independent mental abilities. (3)

Kay Redfield Jamison is another major contributor to the study of the relationship between art and mental illness, specifically manic-depressive illness. In her book, *Touched with Fire*, she emphasizes: "The importance of moods in igniting thought, changing perceptions, creating chaos, forcing order upon that chaos and enabling trans-formation." (4, p. 15)

Her recent study of the poet Robert Lowell, who suffered recurrent debilitating episodes of mania continues this theme: "Mood disorders, depression and bipolar illness occur disproportionally in writers, as well as visual artists and composers. Studying the influence of both normal and pathological moods is critical to understanding how the mind works." (5, p. 5)

Still, the disruptive and disorganizing effect of full-blown mania versus in its milder forms possibly being an engine of creativity remains at issue. Lowell himself commented: "Mania is always in the background" and "It could be pleasant until it gets out of control." (5, p. 129)

This book briefly recounts the lives of a series of great artists and attempts to explicate the extent to which their innovative work was inspired by their personal mental disorders. That most of them possessed 'psychiatric' syndromes of one form or another is clear. The inspirational aspect is the manner in which they adaptively incorporated their psychopathology and their experience of psychic trauma into creating imperishable visual works and, in this process, altered the course of art history and the culture at large.

In 1550, the Florentine painter and architect, Giorgio Vasari, published his monumental *Lives of the Artists*, and essentially invented the discipline of art history. As Bell comments: "On one great canvas Vasari painted a harmonious and glowing composition which sustains with ease the task of conveying the revolutionary nature of what happened in Italian art between the fourteenth and sixteenth centuries." (6)

Simultaneously, Vasari recounted the personal histories of the great artists, including their childhoods and developmental struggles. He did not shy away from observing their mental disturbances and 'eccentricity' and inter-relationship with their creative achievements.

I hope I am following in that searching tradition.

REFERENCES

1) Stendhal: Rome, Naples et Florence en 1817. Voyages en Italie.

2) Kris, E: *Psychoanalytic Explorations in Art.* Schoren Books, New York, 1964.

3) Andreasen, N: *Creativity and Mental Illness: Prevalence Rates in Writers and Their First-Degree Relatives.* American Journal of Psychiatry 144, no. 10 (October, 1987) 1288-92.

4) Jamison, KR: *Touched with Fire. Manic-Depressive Illness and the Artistic Temperament.* Free Press, New York, 1993.

5) Ibid: Robert Lowell: *Setting the River on Fire: A Study of Genius, Mania and Character.* Alfred A Knopf, New York, 2017.

6) Bell, G: Giorgio Vasari: *Lives of the Artists.* The Folio Society, Penguin Books, London, 1993.

7) Rowland, I, Charney N: *The Collector of Lives. Giorgio Vasari and the Invention of Art.* W.W. Norton & Company, New York/London, 2017.

VISIONS: INTRODUCTION

∽∞∾

The four artists discussed in this section all suffered from hallucinatory experiences.

William Blake saw 'visions' from childhood which persisted throughout his adult life. The 'visions' came to suffuse both his poetry and his paintings.

Van Gogh's episodic psychotic illness was beset by hallucinations. Edvard Munch hallucinated that "nature was screaming in my blood" hence the origins of his iconic painting *The Scream*.

Agnes Martin regularly experienced what she called 'trances often precipitated by external stimuli such as listening to Handel's *Messiah* in a church.' She asserted that many of her paintings came to her full-blown as 'visions'.

The relationship between what has been called 'mystical experience', a common hallucinatory experience prevalent in the history of religion and some psychotic states is germane to an understanding of madness and creativity and to these four artists.

Knox in his classic work, *Enthusiasm. A Chapter in the History of Religion* (1) and, by extension, aspects of theological creativity, reviewed the importance of altered states of consciousness as a catalyst for the development of 'enthusiastic' religions. (Blake called himself "an enthusiastic hope-fostered visionary.") Knox recounts how George Fox (1624-1691), one of the founders of Quakerism, had regular ecstatic mystical experiences during which he was overwhelmed by a 'Divine Light'. This experience of the 'Divine Light' as a direct personal manifestation of God became a central doctrinal characteristic of the Quakerism of the 17th century (St Paul was similarly subjected to a 'divine light' on the road to Damascus, leading to his conversion from a Roman tax-collector and persecutor of Christians to one of the most important promulgators of the Christian faith).

John Wesley (1703-1791), the protagonist of the radical revivalist movement within the Anglican Church, also experienced a mystical conversion—a revelation—when depressed, an experience which led to his doctrine of personal salvation by faith alone, which became central to Methodism.

It has been noted clinically that the onset of an acute psychotic episode may be heralded by a state of confusion and acute anxiety, which is then replaced by the psychotic individual's sudden 'understanding' of the 'meaning' of what is happening to them. This 'understanding' may include the belief that the person so afflicted has been chosen to be "God's agent", if not the Messiah, and a conviction that knowledge hidden from others is now in his or her grasp. This sense of *noesis* is often accompanied by a state of exultation.

A representative account of such an episode is found in Morag Coate's description of the onset of her psychosis. (2)

"I got up from where I had been sitting and moved into another room. Suddenly my whole being was filled with light and loveliness and with an upsurge of deeply moving feeling from within myself to meet and reciprocate the influence that flowed into me. I was in a state of the most vivid awareness and illumination. What can I say of it? A cloudless, cerulean blue sky of the mind, shot through with shafts of exquisite, warm dazzling sunlight. In its first and most intense state it lasted perhaps half an hour. It seemed that some force or impulse from without were acting on me, looking into me; that I was in touch with a reality beyond my own; that I had made direct contact with the secret, ultimate source of life. What I had read of the accounts of others acquired suddenly a new meaning. It flashed across my mind, "This is what the mystics mean by the 'direct experience of God'". (p. 21)

The classical mystical experience has usually been interpreted by those who have undergone it as a union with the divine. Though those who have experienced it have often stated that it is ineffable, their descriptions spanning a vast gulf of the time and religion are remarkably consistent. For instance, St Augustine (354-430 CE) at the end of his *Confessions* relates. (3)

"Our conversation had brought us to this point that any pleasure whatsoever of the bodily senses, in any brightness, whatsoever of corporeal light, seemed to us not worthy of comparison with the pleasure of that eternal Light, not worthy even of mention. Rising as our love flamed upward to that selfsame, we passed in review the various levels of bodily things, up to the heavens themselves where sun and moon and stars shine upon this earth. And brighter still we soared, thinking in our minds and speaking and marveling at Your works: and so we came to our own souls, and went beyond them to come at last to the region of richness unending where you feed Israel forever with the food of truth: and there life is that wisdom by which all things are made, both the things that have been and the things that are to be." (p. 164)

Mystical experience, not *ipso facto*, a manifestation of psychosis *per se*, has a 'creative' aspect – making something transcendent and meaningful out of a potentially overwhelming altered state of consciousness.

Michael Pollan's recent analysis and review of the history of psychedelic drug use both in other cultures (*cf. The Flesh of the Gods* by Terence McKenna. (4)) and in America also speaks to mystical experience. (Pollan himself acts like an anthropologist participant – observer in imbibing various psychedelics in different settings and relating his subjective experience.) (5)

For some who take a psychedelic agent the 'classical' mystical experience may occur as a consequence. Pollan notes: "According to scholars of mysticism, these shared traits generally include a vision of unity in which all things, including the self are subsumed (expressed in the phrase "All is One"; a sense of certainty about what one has perceived ("Knowledge has been revealed to me"); feelings of joy, blessedness and satisfaction; a transcendence of the categories we rely on to organize the world, such as time and space or self and other; a sense that whatever has been apprehended is somehow sacred... and often paradoxical (so while the self may vanish, awareness abides.) Last is the conviction that the experience is ineffable." (5, p. 285)

The four artists described in this section all speak to aspects of this altered state of consciousness experience and its expression in their art.

REFERENCES

1) Knox, RA: *Enthusiam. A Chapter in the History of Religion.* Oxford: Oxford University Press, 1950.
2) Coate, M: *Beyond All Reason.* J.P. Lippincott, New York, 1965.
3) St Augustine: Confessions. Translated by F.K. Sheed. Sheed and Ward, New York, 1943.
4) McKenna, Terence: *Food of the Gods: The Search for the Original Tree of Knowledge.* New York, Bantam Books, 1992.
5) Pollan, M: *How to Change Your Mind.* Penguin Press, New York, 2018.
6) James, William: *The Varieties of Religious Experience E-book.* Project Guttenberg, 2014.

WILLIAM BLAKE (1757–1827)

❦

TO SEE A WORLD IN A GRAIN OF SAND

William Blake was both a great poet and a great painter. Blake invented a method of relief engraving that was able to combine his poetry and paintings so that they formed a unified work. In the West, only Michelangelo had demonstrated such singular talent in both painting and poetry, but he did not combine them. This artistic combination found in Blake's work occurred regularly in classical Chinese art wherein landscapes and narrative scrolls were frequently accompanied by the artist's poems superimposed on the paintings.

As Sampson (1, p. xvii) noted: "By far the greater number of Blake's works were produced by his own discovery, which he terms 'illuminated printing', a name suggestive of the manner in which, as in medieval manuscripts, text and design are interwoven into a single artistic harmony… In this process, the text and surrounding pictorial embellishments were executed in some species of varnish upon copper plates, which were afterwards etched in a bath of acid until the whole design stood in relief as on a stereotype. From these plates impressions were printed in various schemes of monochrome and afterwards delicately tinted by the artist in washes of water-color, each copy thus possessing an individuality of its own." (1, p. xvii)

Blake himself believed that the secret of this new mode of printing was revealed to him in a 'vision' by the spirit of his favorite brother Robert who died in 1787 of tuberculosis.

The experience of 'visions' was a central part of Blake's life. From childhood onwards he saw 'visions'. His biographer Bentley recounts: "Once his mother beat him for running in and saying he saw the Prophet Ezekiel under a tree in the field." (2, p. 19) Blake is thus in a long tradition of mystics whom throughout recorded history have experienced hallucinatory 'revelatory' experiences. For Blake, they persisted throughout his life. His wife commented in 1810, "I have very little of Mr. Blake's company; he is always in Paradise." Blake's recurrent 'visions' suffused his poetry and painting, especially his great epics such as *Visions of the Daughters of Albion*, and *Europe a Prophecy* with its iconic frontispiece *The Ancient of Days* (original unique prints of this image exist in the Glasgow University library, the British Museum and Library of Congress).

Blake was one of the progenitors of the revolutionary 18th century Romantic movement in poetry and his verse was admired by Coleridge and Wordsworth.

Stanzas by Blake such as the following have become an imperishable part of the Western canon: "To see a world in a grain of sand / And a heaven in a wild flower / Hold infinity in the palm of your hand / And eternity in an hour." – from *Auguries of Innocence*" Long before Heinz Kohut and self-psychology, Blake captured the essential tragedy of narcissistic pathology: "Love seeketh only self to please / To bind another to its delight / Joys in another's loss of ease / And builds a hell in heaven's despite." – from *The Clod and the Pebble*.

Blake was the third of six children. His father was a draper who owned a hosiery and haberdashery shop in London. As was common for tradesmen, the family lived above the shop. Blake was raised in the Protestant Dissenting tradition, one that emphasized private devotion and individual conscience, separate from the authority of priest and church. In the lexicon of the 18th century, the term for extreme dissent was "enthusiasm" (possessed by God). Later in life, Blake, who was deeply religious, referred to himself as "an enthusiastic hope-fostered visionary."

According to Bentley, (2) Blake's father was "a gentle amiable man" and his mother "a tender and sympathetic" person. He notes, however, "She was capable of beating her children under severe provocation such as a willful lie. (However), her strange son William was privately encouraged to make designs and in the solitude of his room he used to make drawings and illustrate these with verses, to be hung up together in his mother's chamber."

Already in childhood with his mother's active encouragement his vocation had been set. Blake was most attached to his younger brother Robert. "William thought of Robert as a fellow spirit." (2, p. 6) In Blake's *Milton* engravings long after Robert's demise, he made images of the two of them receiving the "inspiration" of Milton.

'Visions' as mentioned earlier were a persistent element of Blake's life. When he was ten visiting his grandfather's house he saw a tree filled with angels. However, he simultaneously demonstrated artistic and literary ability from an early age and his enlightened parents enrolled him in a drawing school at the age of ten. He was further educated as a commercial engraver and was later admitted because of his artistic talent to the prestigious Royal Academy, overseen by the great 18th century portraitist, Sir Joshua Reynolds, whom Blake came to despise for his conventional approach to art.

In 1782, Blake married Catherine Boucher, the illiterate daughter of a market-gardener. She believed in all his 'visions' This was to prove to be a devoted albeit childless marriage. For Blake: "My wife is like a flame of many colors, of precious jewels." Some of her effect on Blake with his racing mind was therapeutic: "He fancied that while she looked on him, as he worked, her sitting quite still by his side, doing nothing soothed his tempestuous mind." (2, p. 70)

Blake's artistic career was checkered although he had a number of aristocratic patrons who recognized his genius.

In 1800 Blake descended into, as he describes it, "a deep pit of melancholy. Melancholy, without any real reason for it." (2, p. 207) However, this was followed by periods of "Illumination" during which he created his mystical *Auguries of Innocence* (1803).

It is most likely that Blake had a recurrent bi-polar illness, albeit a mild form that did not disrupt, and may have enhanced his transcendent artistic vision. "A fearful symmetry" indeed, as he stated in: "Tiger! Tiger! Burning bright / In the forests of the night / What immortal hand or eye / Could frame thy fearful symmetry?"

Blake died in 1827, possibly of liver failure secondary to biliary cirrhosis induced by chronic copper ingestion from working on his engraving. He wrote: "If the doors of perception were cleansed everything would appear to man as it is, infinite."

For Blake, the great artist in both poetry and painting, the doors of perception were indeed cleansed both by his genius and possibly his affective disorder.

REFERENCES

1) *The Poetical Works of William Blake* Edited by Sampson J. Oxford University Press, London and New York, reprinted in 1961.

2) Bentley, GE: *The Stranger from Paradise*. A biography of William Blake. Yale University Press, New Haven and London, 2001.

3) William Blake. *The Complete Illuminated Books*. Thames and Hudson, New York, 2000.

VINCENT VAN GOGH (1853–1890)

❦

EXPERIENCING MADNESS

Vincent Van Gogh's paintings, etchings, and drawings represent a pinnacle of post-Impressionist modern art. Produced in a brief ten years from the embrace of his identity as an artist at age 27 until his suicide in 1890, his work later achieved iconic status.

His paintings are instantly recognizable by their swirling lines, unique composition, turbulent brush strokes and intense startling juxtaposition of colors. Visual and emotional engagement with the natural world from childhood until his death was central to his artistic inspiration. (1)

Van Gogh was not only a great painter, essentially unrecognized in his life-time, he was a brilliant writer. He bequeathed us a remarkable body of correspondence that provides considerable insight into his mental life and his poignant, tragic struggle with the psychotic illness that was to claim his life. (2)

In April 1889 he wrote, "what consoles me a little is that I'm beginning to consider madness as an illness like any other and accept the thing as it is, while during the actual crisis it seemed to me that everything I was imagining was reality." (2, p. 656)

Van Gogh was the oldest of six children. His father was a protestant pastor in rural Holland. Vincent initially attended a village school and then spent several years at a boarding school. His relationship with his family, especially his father, was fraught because he repudiated what he perceived as his parents' rigid, moralistic and conventional beliefs. His younger brother Theo, who became a successful art dealer, was a positive and crucially emotional support in Vincent's life. It was Theo who suggested to Vincent, based on what he had perspicaciously seen in Vincent's early sketches and drawings, that he dedicate himself to being an artist. Vincent's previous attempted vocation as a mendicant itinerant preacher identifying with the poor had not gone well. Vincent's letters to Theo are psychologically revealing. They are redolent with self-preoccupations, critical and perceptive artistic commentary all directed to the listening, empathic and caring brother:

"There's a bond between you and me which time can only strengthen if we press on with the work, and that is art..."
(2, p. 375)

At the age of 16, thanks to an uncle's intervention, Vincent was introduced to the commercial art world and began working at the firm of *Goupil and Cie* which specialized in the sale of artistic reproductions. This employment provided a considerable education for Vincent in the visual arts. Theo also worked for this firm initially in Brussels and later in The Hague. After a brief stint in the firm's offices in London and then a transfer to Paris, Vincent's employment was terminated in 1875. Ostensibly, this was because he neglected his duties. In reality, he had become obsessively preoccupied with religion and Bible studies. His parents expressed concern over his "religious obsession" which may have been, as it often is, a prodromal manifestation of what would later be his more fulminant illness. In 1877, in a letter to Theo, one sees hints of this: "My head is often hot and my thoughts are confused." (2, p. 89)

In 1875, Vincent wrote to Theo a *cri-de-cœur*: "Man is not placed on this Earth merely to be happy; nor is he placed here merely to be honest, he is here to accomplish great things, to arrive at nobleness and to outgrow the vulgarity in which all individuals drag on." (2, p. 53)

The same year he wrote to Theo: "Feeling even a fine feeling for the beauty of nature isn't the same as religious feeling although I believe the two are closely connected. The same is true of a feeling for art." (2, p. 56)

From 1880 to 1883, Van Gogh turned away from his "religious fanaticism," which had been to such a degree that his pastor-father had contemplated the hospitalization of his son, to educating himself technically as an artist. During this period he became intimate with a prostitute who was his regular model. This liaison resulted in a brief hospitalization for the treatment of the acute venereal disease he contracted.

Simultaneously he was developing a theory of color based on his observations of nature, one that would infuse his paintings and give them their singular quality: "out of the ground shoot young beech trees that catch the light on one side – are brilliantly green there – and then shaded sides of those trunks are warm, strong, and black-green. Beyond these trunks, beyond the brown-red ground, is a sky, a very delicate blue-grey, warm – almost not blue – sparkling". (2, p. 260)

By 1886, Van Gogh was living with Theo in Paris. As Jansen, Luitjen and Bakker note: "Artists with whom Vincent came into contact in this period reported that he was easily upset, aired his opinions whether they were called for or not, and always seemed to be looking for an argument". (2, p. 20) In 1888, he left Paris for

Provence, whose intense Mediterranean light was transformative for his art. Here, in the South of France, he would create many imperishable masterpieces.

Vincent and Theo both admired the radical paintings of Paul Gauguin. Vincent invited Gauguin to share a studio in Provence which, in Vincent's mind was to be an innovative ground-breaking "Studio of the South." Shortly after Gauguin's arrival the relationship between the two artists rapidly deteriorated. Vincent was particularly irked by Gauguin's effortless mastery of the denizens of the local brothels. Three months into their time together, Vincent became floridly psychotic, threatened Gauguin's life, amputated his own ear and was hospitalized.

Van Gogh would spend the next year of his life in the asylum of *Saint-Rémy* where he suffered intermittent psychotic episodes. In a period of lucidity he wrote to Theo: "Anyway my dear fellow, we must accept it, the illnesses of our time, all in all it's only fair that having lived for years in relatively good health, sooner or later we have our share of them. As for me, you'll feel a little that I wouldn't have chosen madness if there had been a choice but one can't catch it anymore." (2, p. 657)

During his time in this benign and progressive institution, Vincent's custodians provided him with a studio and encouraged his painting. While there he painted his classic *Starry Night* (now in the Museum of Modern Art, New York City). He was beset, however by recurrent psychotic episodes. He wrote: "I cannot possibly describe what the thing I have is like; there are terrible fits of anxiety – without any apparent cause – or then again a feeling of emptiness and fatigue in the mind. I consider the whole rather as a simple accident, no doubt a large part of it is my fault, and from time to time I have fits of melancholy, atrocious remorse." (2, p. 661)

His correspondence with Theo was of critical positive therapeutic importance. "Your kind letter did me good today". (1, p. 661) The constant blows to his self-esteem engendered by his illness are captured in a letter to his sister: "It's quite odd perhaps that the result of this terrible attack is that in my mind there's hardly any really clear desire or hope left, and I am wondering if it is thus that one thinks when with the passions somewhat extinguished, one comes down the mountain instead of climbing it." (2, p. 666)

Van Gogh was comforted by his acute awareness that those around him in the asylum shared elements of his disorder: "speaking of my condition, I'm still so grateful for yet another thing, I observe in others that, like me, they too have heard sounds and strange voices during their crises, that things appeared to change before their eyes. And that softens the horror that I retained at first of the crisis I had and which comes to you unexpectedly, cannot but frighten you beyond measure. Once one knows that its part of the illness one takes it like other things. Had I not seen other mad people at close hand I wouldn't have been able to rid myself of thinking about it all the time." (2, p. 671)

Aware that effective somatic medical treatments for his illness were non-existent, he shrewdly observed the therapeutic potential of the doctor-patient relationship: "...the doctors... do you know what they can do all the same – they give you a more cordial handshake, greater than many hands, and their presence can really be very pleasant and reassuring sometimes." (2, p. 661)

By 1890, Van Gogh was eager to leave the asylum, but possessed sufficient insight to recognize that he needed a physician who would continue to monitor his case. He moved to *Auvers-sur-Oise*, a rural village north of Paris and placed himself in the care of Dr. Paul Gachet whom he subsequently painted in a series of now-famous portraits. To Theo he wrote: "Anyway, père Gachet is a lot, yes a lot like you."

(2, p. 780) "Then I've found in Dr. Gachet a ready-made friend and something like a new brother would be… he's very nervous and very bizarre himself. I did his portrait the other day." (2, p. 781) While in Auvers-sur-Oise he commented: "Ah, if I'd been able to work without this bloody illness! How many things I could have done, isolated from the others, according to what the land would tell me. But – yes – this journey is well and truly finished." (2, p. 730) An ominous note given what was about to occur. In July 1890, Van Gogh went to paint in the fields outside Auvers and then proceeded to shoot himself in the chest. He died two days later.

Van Gogh's voyage through madness and its tragic outcome together with his extraordinary artistic achievement pose many questions. Are his illness and his unique creativity linked or was his psychosis an adventitious and destructive element that recurrently derailed his artistic genius? His letters suggest the later.

A recent exhibit and conference at *The Van Gogh Museum* in Amsterdam called *On the Verge of Insanity* focused on this issue. (3) Various diagnostic hypothesis were promulgated including digitalis toxicity to explain his intense use of the color yellow and the presence of haloes in his last paintings. This was based on his portraits of Dr. Gachet holding a fox-glove plant and the assumption that Gachet prescribed it to his patient as it was used then in the treatment of epilepsy – another putative diagnosis for Van Gogh. However it seems most likely to this author that Van Gogh suffered from a recurrent bi-polar illness which at times may have intensified perception and thus found its way into the intense and unusual use of color in his paintings. However the disorder, as he eloquently expressed, was inimicable to his heroic creative achievements.

REFERENCES

1) *Van Gogh and nature.* Catalogue of an exhibition at The Clark Art Institute, 2015. Distributed by Yale University Press. New Haven and London, 2015.

2) Vincent Van Gogh. *Ever Yours. The Essential Letters.* Edited by Jansen, L., Luitjen H., and Bakker, N. Yale University Press, New Haven and London, 2014.

3) *On the Verge of Insanity: Van Gogh and his illness*, Van Gogh Museum, Amsterdam. Reviewed in the Guardian, 12 July 2016.

EDVARD MUNCH (1863–1944)

∽⊗∽

ANGUISH AND SCREAMING

Edvard Munch's painting *The Scream* (1893, now in the Munch Museum, Oslo) is his most famous work capturing, as it does, in its intense colors, evoked horror and expressionist form, a moment of mental and existential break-down that has become a symbol of universal human anxiety. This iconic image exists in two paintings, two pastels and a number of lithographs. Of its personal psychological origins, Munch wrote: "I was walking down the road with two friends when the sun set: suddenly the sky turned as red as blood. I stopped and leaned against the fence, feeling unspeakably tired. Tongues of fire and blood stretched over the bluish black fjord. My friends went on walking, while I lagged behind shivering with fear. Then I heard the enormous infinite scream of nature." (1, p. 17)

Later he commented: "...for several years I was almost mad... You know my picture *The Scream*? I was stretched to the limit... nature was screaming in my blood... After that I gave up hope of ever being able to love again." (1, p. 152)

Despite Munch's confession to being 'almost mad', for most of his life he had a long successful career as a painter and achieved considerable recognition and ultimately fame.

In the early stages of his career, he was regarded as a *Symbolist*. The late 19th century symbolist movement in both visual arts and music rejected naturalism and realism and privileged spirituality, the imagination, mythology and dream-states. In this tradition, Munch's work frequently involves themes of death, social isolation and psychic distress. His paintings are haunting and often emotionally disturbing. His thematic elements and his intense use of color, combined with dark forbidding shadows evocative of the underworld influenced the later German expressionists such as George Grosz and Otto Dix.

The contemporary Norwegian writer Karl Ove Knausgaard notes in an essay accompanying a recent exhibition of Munch's late works: "Munch lived until he was eighty, and he painted almost every day… and more or less in isolation for the first thirty years. The most incredible thing about Edvard Munch is that he produced such a phenomenal amount of work and he did it on his own. He had no children, and apart from a few difficult relationships in his youth, he had no wife or lovers and he kept the few friends he had at a distance. The only thing he did was paint." (2, p. 14)

In the same catalogue, Bischoff notes: "…what makes Munch's art so essentially distinctive is not his presentation of important childhood experiences, nor his acute psychological perceptions. Rather his significance is a matter of radical artistic approach both of composition and painting technique. *The Dead Mother and the Child* painted in 1897-1899 and now in Oslo's Munch Museum may serve as an example of his radical approach… Again we are in the death chamber. The scene recalls the early death of young Edvard's mother in 1868. Beyond the bed, which is positioned horizontally in the composition, we see five adult members of the family, evidently

26

helpless in the face of death as we can tell from their nervous gestures and restless movements, but in the foreground this side of the mother's bed is young Sophie (Munch's elder sister) then six years old and one year older than Edvard, holding her hands over her ears to block out the silent but painful scream of death."

Munch was the second of five children. His father was a doctor whose career was problematic so that the family lived in impoverished circumstances. His mother died of tuberculosis when he was five, as did his sister Sophie, when Edvard was fourteen. These premature deaths were to haunt Munch's life and art.

About his father, he wrote: "My father was temperamentally nervous and obsessively religious. From him I inherited the seeds of madness." (3, p. 7)

When he was 19, he enrolled in college in Kristiania (now Oslo) to study engineering, but left after a year to pursue a career as an artist much to his father's chagrin. He became a student at the Royal School of Art and Design. He flirted in his early work with impressionism, but soon embraced a more radical and original style. He spent time in Paris and was influenced by the work he saw there by Gauguin and Van Gogh. He then spent four years in Berlin where his mature style crystallized. In 1897 he returned to Kristiania having by that time received critical approval. However, his romantic life was fraught with a dramatic, unhappy love-affair, and he was drinking heavily. By 1908 his mental state, always precarious, was deteriorating and as he wrote: "My condition was verging on madness – it was touch and go." (3, p. 236)

He was admitted to a psychiatric clinic in Berlin for eight months where the milieu and psychological treatment stabilized him. Upon discharge he bought a country-estate outside of Kristiania where he lived, in relative solitude, the rest of his life. He continued to produce remarkable paintings as the centerpiece of a recent exhibition in

New York attests. One of his last paintings: *Between the Clock and the Bed* is a self-portrait. It brilliantly captures old age, mortality and approaching death, the latter theme running through his whole oeuvre. In this painting, it is highly personalized as he realizes time is now running out for him.

For Munch, it is my thesis that his painting was profoundly 'therapeutic' and held his mental illness in relative check. As Munch himself wrote: "My art has been an act of confession." (2, p. 11) One which prevented the demons from overwhelming him.

REFERENCES

1) Prideaux, S: *Edvard Munch: Behind the Scream*. Yale University Press, New Haven and London, 2005.
2) Edvard Munch: *Between the Clock and the Bed*. Catalogue of an exhibit. Metropolitan Museum of Art, New York, 2017.
3) Eggum, A: *Edvard Munch*. C.N. Potter, New York, 1984.
4) Gill, HJ (Ed): *The Private Journals of Edvard Munch: We Are Flames Which pour out of the Earth*. University of Wisconsin Press, Madison, Wisconsin, 2005.

AGNES MARTIN (1912–2004)

◠◠◠

TRANCES AND SPIRITUAL GRIDS

Abstract art was not invented in the West. Many non-Western cultures have a centuries-long tradition of non-representational art that suffuses their ceramics, textiles and architecture.

Dickerman observed that the advent of Western abstract art in the early 20th century: "presented paintings that differed from almost all of those that had proceeded them in the long history of the medium in the Western tradition: shunning the depiction of objects in the world they displayed works with no discernable subject matter. Indeed, they abandoned the premise of making a picture of something." (1, p. 13)

The conventional narrative of the origins of abstract art in the West valorizes Wassily Kandinsky, Kazimir Malevich and Piet Mondrian as the seminal figures in this upheaval. Kandinsky was central to the process. As Whitford commented, Kandinsky "did not invent abstract art, but he was its most consistent and consequential pioneer. He was also the first to give abstraction a coherent theoretical foundation. In numerous essays and two books he defined a basic pictorial language of pure colors and form and suggested what it could be made to communicate and how." (2, p. 12)

This narrative of the origin of abstract art in the West has been turned on its head by the re-discovery of the late 19th century Swedish painter Hilma af Klint who some five years before Kandinsky was creating abstract painting, as a recent exhibition at the Guggenheim Museum in New York City demonstrates. (3) As Peter Schjeldahl comments: "On her own terms, she operated outside time... She was channeling visions received from a spirit world." (4) Born in 1862 near Stockholm she attended the Swedish Royal Academy of Fine Arts. Since the age of 17, she had been attending séances. In 1896, she founded *The Five* with four other women. As Schjeldahl notes: "At regular séances they received messages from supernatural 'High Masters' which they documented in notebooks... The spirits had identities; Amaliel, Clemens, Esther, Georg and Gregor." (4) Further Amaliel gave af Klint a 'commission' for her work, monumental canvases painted between 1903-1907, to be displayed in a specially-constructed 'temple' for which Frank Lloyd Wright's New York Guggenheim Museum in New York City seems a particularly apt venue today. Af Klint never married and insisted that her work was not to be displayed until twenty years after her death, possibly imagining that only then could it be appreciated. (She died in 1944 at the age of 82.) In one sense af Klint was the first 'outsider' artist living in her own hermetic spiritually-infused creative world.

Agnes Martin is an heir to some elements of Hilma af Klint's practice. Two years ago, Martin had a posthumous solo exhibition of her singular abstract art at the very same Guggenheim Museum which some commentators felt had distinctly 'mystical' overtones. (5)

Though Martin is recognized as one of the greatest practitioners of late 20th century abstract art, she eschewed such a categorization and declaimed: "I would like my work to be recognized as being in the classic tradition (Coptic, Egyptian, Greek, Chinese) as representing the ideal in the mind." (6, p. 37)

Her biographer, Princenthal, observed: "Composed of the simplest elements, including ruled penciled lines and a narrow range of forms – grids, stripes, and very occasionally circles, they reveal an aesthetic sense that is the equivalent of perfect pitch." (7, p. 7)

Martin averred that her paintings came to her as "visions" complete in every detail. She suffered throughout her adult life from a recurrent fulminant psychotic illness that sometimes landed her in the hospital. Martin referred to her psychotic episodes as "trances". She related to a friend: "I was in a perfect small church on Second Avenue in New York at Christmas time and hearing the *Messiah*. After three notes, I zonked out – in a trance – I've been in many trances, you know. That's how they put me away in Bellevue." (8, p. 159) The psychiatrist who treated her from 1985 to 2000 when she was living and working in New Mexico, commented on "the depth of sensitivity with which she was able to make art in the face of a disorder that for many people would be devastating." (7, p. 159)

Martin was born in the prairies of Saskatchewan. "My grandparents on both side came from Scotland and they went to the prairie in covered wagons – my parents were also pioneers." (9, p. 1) One could speculate that an awareness of the prairies of her childhood and her family heritage, with their vast grids of wheat-fields, catalyzed her distinctive abstract style. Her father died when she was two years old and her family moved to Vancouver. Martin was the third of four children. Somewhat tellingly, Martin said of her mother that she "didn't like children and she hated me, God how she hated me." (7, p. 24) As a teenager she was a talented, competitive swimmer and invited participant in Olympic trials. Moving to Washington state as a young adult, she obtained a teaching certificate and worked in various rural schools. In 1941 she left for New York City, where she enrolled at Columbia's Teacher's College and took courses in studio art. In the late 1940s she moved to New Mexico and began painting.

Martin returned to New York City in 1957 and became a member of an artistic community that included Jasper Johns, Elsworth Kelly and Robert Rauschenberg at Coenties Slip, a waterfront district in lower Manhattan, where she obtained a studio. This was an extremely influential and mutually supportive group of artists, all friends of Martin, who were initiating a new wave of both abstraction and minimalism. In some sense this group of artists, all of whom would become renowned, were also 'outsiders' since they were openly gay at a repressive time when such sexual orientation engendered perilous societal and professional opprobrium. Martin's romantic attachments were with other women. Princenthal notes: "She refused the label lesbian (as she did the term feminist when it was applied to her). In her life, as in her work, renunciation was as important as embrace." (7, p. 11) By 1964, Martin had developed her characteristic "grid" paintings. Simultaneously, Martin became fascinated by Zen Buddhism and mystical experience, in particular the recorded "visions" of St Teresa of Avila (1552-1581). In 1967 following another acute psychotic episode and hospitalization, she left New York. Later she stated: "I left New York because every day I suddenly felt I wanted to die and it was connected to painting." (7, p. 147) By this time she had received considerable critical appreciation for her spare, minimalist but evocative paintings which bordered on the mystical in their subtlety and purity.

For over a year, Martin led a lonely peripatetic life travelling in a camper in the Pacific Northwest. She finally settled in New Mexico and personally built a studio and home on a remote isolated mesa. She resumed painting and her considerable output from this period is considered her most significant. She lived the rest of her life there and died at age 92 of congestive heart failure.

An eloquent writer, she articulated her spiritual and artistic credo in a poetic piece entitled *The Untroubled Mind*: "People think that painting is about color / It's mostly composition / It's composition that's the whole thing / The classic image – / Two late Tang dishes, one with a flower image, one empty – The empty form goes all the way to heaven / It is the classic form – lighter weight." (9)

Through her art, Martin conquered the demons of her psychosis and achieved a type of creative tranquility and transcendence, embodied in her remarkable art.

REFERENCES

1) Dickerman, L: *Inventing Abstraction 1910-1925. How a Radical Idea Changed Modern Art.* Catalogue of the exhibit, Museum of Modern Art, 2013.

2) Whitford, P: Kandinsky: *Watercolors and Other Works on Paper.* London, Thames & Hudson 1999.

3) Hilma af Klint: *Paintings for the Future.* Catalogue of an Exhibition at the Guggenheim Museum, 2018.

4) Schjeldahl, P: *Out of Time,* The New Yorker, Oct 22, 2018.

5) Agnes Martin. Catalogue of an exhibition, Guggenheim Museum, New York, 2017.

6) Agnes Martin (Exhibition Catalogue) Vienna, Hochschule fur Angewandte, Kunst 1997.

7) Princenthal, N: Agnes Martin: *Her Life and Art,* New York, Thames & Hudson, 2015.

8) Glimcher: Agnes Martin: *Paintings, Writings, Remembrances,* London, Phaidon 2012.

9) Hashel, B. Agnes Martin (Exhibition Catalogue) New York, Whitney Museum of American Art, 1992.

VIOLENCE: INTRODUCTION

Violence, alas, runs through human history, society and behavior like a red thread. A manifestation of human aggression which is protean in its expression through war, murder, suicide and sexual assault.

The artists discussed in this section all exhibited some aspects of violent behavior. Caravaggio was literally a murderer. Pollock was prone to violent outbursts often fueled by alcohol. Rothko's calculated suicide accomplished by slicing his brachial arteries in the bath while at the height of his fame was a quintessential violent act.

The history of art and artists, like most history, is redolent with violence. Benvenuto Cellini (1500-1571) is a case in point. A talented Florentine Mannerist sculptor and goldsmith best known for the *Cellini Salt Cellar* (now in the Kunsthistorisches Museum in Vienna) and the bronze monumental statue *Perseus with the Head of Medusa* (possibly his greatest work). Commissioned by the Medici Grand Duke Cosimo, it was designed to testify to the wealth and stability of Cosimo's regime, which consolidated political power over 16th century Tuscany and negotiated the withdrawal of the Spanish from the region. This great bronze statue vied with Donatello's much earlier *Judith* and Michelangelo's *David* to dominate the Piazza della Signoria in Florence. All three creations were symbolic testimony meant to signify Renaissance Florence's political cultural and intellectual superiority.

Cellini wrote a remarkable memoir of his life: *The Autobiography* (1) which, prudently, given its racy and often scurrilous nature, he did not publish in his lifetime. Cellini stated at the beginning "all men of whatever quality they be, who have done anything exceptional or which may properly be deemed exceptional, ought, if they are persons of truth and honesty, to describe their life in their own hand." (2, p. 11) This was when he was fifty-six. As Pope-Hennessy notes "there was every reason why in July 1557 Cellini should have sought the consolation of reliving the past. In the previous February he had been condemned to four years' imprisonment for sodomy and the sentence had been reduced to confinement in his own house." (2, p. 11)

Cellini was named 'Benvenuto' ('Welcome') because his parents' marriage was for many years childless, and when he was delivered his father Giovanni exclaimed: "Lord, I thank thee with my whole heart; this child is very dear to me. *Si il benvenuto.*" (2, p. 23)

Cellini's life history is filled with violent behavior – brawls, murders (at least three), sexual assault and theft. Naturally he often ran afoul of the law and was prosecuted. He was often rescued by noble patrons who wished to employ him. The parallel with Caravaggio is hard to resist. Like Caravaggio he was a great artist, and it should be noted that they both lived in a society that was notably violent as was Elizabethan England during the same time period, so this phenomenon was not confined to Italy in the 16th century.

Cellini was bi-sexual and had multiple mistresses and lovers. It is clear that he was filled with energy, both creative and frankly carnal, which one could view as bordering on the hypo-manic. He did not die prematurely as Caravaggio did. As Pope-Hennessy observes the Florentine Academia del Disegno on his death "came into his own. On 15 February Messer Benvenuto Cellini, sculptor – on his own instruction was buried in our Chapel of the Annunziata, with great funeral pomp, in which the whole of our Academy and the Company took part' (2, p. 284)

Another example of frenzied violent behavior in an artist is to be found in an episode in the life history of Gian Lorenzo Bernini (1598-1680) though the episode is isolated and propelled by jealous rage and is not recurrently typical of Bernini's behavior.

More than anyone else, through his designs of churches, chapels, public squares (notably his grand Colonnade in St Peter's Square) and secular buildings, his imprint made Rome the beautiful Baroque city it remains today. Some would also say he was the greatest Baroque sculptor. His *Saint Teresa in Ecstasy* in the church of Santa Maria della Vittoria is a startling magnificent masterpiece. St Teresa of Avila (1515-1592) described a vision in which she was repeatedly penetrated by the spear of an angel "I saw in his hands a long golden spear. This he plunged into my heart.... The pain was so severe that it made me utter several moans, and yet such pain was exceedingly sweet that one cannot possibly desire it to cease". (3)

The sexual connotations of this are obvious and Bernini creates an extraordinary work embodying both a spiritual 'vision' and an orgasm. It is one of the greatest and powerful sculptures of the Baroque period.

With regard to the episode of murderous violence, Bernini in the 1630s began an affair with a married woman, Constanza Bonarelli (later portrayed by him in a famous bust now in the Museo Nazionale del Bargello, Florence). He became enraged when he discovered that his brother Luigi, who worked in Bernini's atelier was also having an affair with Costanza. Bernini's biographer, Franco Mormando (3) notes: "the crushing sight that then greeted Bernini's eyes was that of Luigi exiting the house with a half-dressed Costanza, who was there at the door saying good-bye to her lover with whom she had spent the night. Bernini went berserk. Reeling in shock by so profound a betrayal, he went off in mad pursuit of his brother.... He had also made provisions for an appropriate revenge on his faithless mistress: he ordered one of his servants to go to Costanza pretending to bring her a gift of two bottles of wine. In presenting Costanza with the wine, the servant was, at the convenient moment to slash her face with a razor. The servant found Costanza still in bed... and the act of revenge was carried out just as orchestrated by Bernini. The face-slashing strikes us today as a shocking act of monstrous violence.... Fortunately Bernini was prevented from killing his brother. Luigi was wise enough to flee Rome immediately, eventually ending up in Bologna." (3, pp. 103-105) Bernini's mother Angelina wrote a poignant letter to Cardinal Francesco Barberini indicting her son's personality as narcissistic and psychopathic and asking him to intervene and prevent fratricide. This appeal was successful and Pope Urban VIII (Matteo Barbarini) "suggested" i.e. "ordered" that Bernini marry and relent from promiscuous activity. Bernini did so and went on to a long and productive artistic career transforming the city of Rome.

Nonetheless, this act of violence is telling and speaks to the potential violence in the creative artist.

Edgar Degas (1834-1912) the great French painter who defined himself as a "realist" not an "impressionist" gave expression to this theme in two statements: "A picture is a thing which requires as much knavery, as much malice, and as much vice as the perpetration of a crime" and "Art is vice. You don't marry it legitimately, you rape it". (4)

Degas notwithstanding, one could speculate that 'violence' is inimical to great creative endeavors and is an adventitious and malignant byproduct of the intense creative energy that underpins the work of the artists described in this section and thus leads to their downfall.

REFERENCES

1) *The Autobiography of Benvenuto Cellini.* Translated by George Bull, Penguin Books, London 1956.
2) Pope-Hennessy, J: *Cellini.* Abeville Press, New York, 1985.
3) Mormando, F: *Bernini: His Life and His Rome*, University of Chicago Press, Chicago and London, 2013.
4) *The Shop-Talk of Edgar Degas.* R.H. Ives Grammell, ed. University Press, Boston, 1961.

CARAVAGGIO (1571–1610)

∞

PRINCE OF DARKNESS

The relatively easy art excursion in Tuscany, beginning in Arezzo passing through Monterchi and San Sepolcro, ending in Urbino, is known as *The Piero della Francesca Trail*. It encompasses almost all of the artist's works that are *in situ*.

In his eponymous book, the art-critic Pope-Hennessy comments concerning Della Francesca: "There comes a point in life when the artists one has known cease to be objects of research and become friends. The workings of their minds assume a taken-for-granted quality that transcends art-historical analysis… Let there be no mistake about it, Piero is a reclusive, silent rather taciturn friend." (1, p. 13)

Della Francesca was born about 1420 in Borgo San Sepolcro, a small town in Tuscany and remained there his whole life. Now acknowledged as one of the greatest artists of the Italian Renaissance (his reputation languished in obscurity until his 'rediscovery' in the late 19th century.) His work, when directly experienced has a powerful impact on the viewer.

What is known of Della Francesca's personal history in its tranquility and small geographical range is in striking contrast to that of Michelangelo Merisi da Caravaggio who is Della Francesca's equal in both artistic genius and ability to engage the viewer in a powerful psychological dialogue.

It is relatively simple for the art-traveler to visit Della Francesca's masterpieces. *The Caravaggio Trail* is another matter. It requires the traveler to journey from Rome to Naples, to Malta, and finally Sicily to see his *in situ* works. This geographical range is no accident and reflects the tempestuous psychology and wildly impulsive character of Caravaggio as he escaped from place-to-place, painting brilliant works in each venue and then fleeing after some felony, pursued by ecclesiastical, law-enforcement and political authorities.

Violence and blood permeate Caravaggio's life and are expressed in his art which transformed western painting. He introduced a new visual dynamism to painting that he combined with a highly developed naturalism. Unlike most painters of his time, he used real models drawn from the streets, a practice that enhanced his naturalism. His paintings captured people in moments of intense psychological tension, and his use of raking light and deep shadow was dramatic and original. His innovative paintings and use of *chiaroscuro* influenced the later work of Velazquez and Rembrandt. Peter Paul Rubens (1577-1640) was a great admirer and incorporated Caravaggio's original use of light and dark into some of his dramatic works.

As the art-historian David Stone observes: "No stranger to fusing the diabolical and the creative as a metaphor for artistic… Caravaggio invented one of the most brilliant conceits in Seicento art when he signed his name in the 'blood' oozing from the Baptist's severed neck in his picture for the Knights of Malta, *The Beheading of Saint John the Baptist*." (2, p. 572) (Now in the Church of St John Valleta, Malta.)

Graham-Dixon states: "Caravaggio's art is made from darkness and light. His pictures present spot-lit moments of extreme and often agonized human experience. A man is decapitated in his bedchamber, blood spurting from a deep gash in his neck. A man is assassinated on the high altar of a church. A woman is shot in the stomach with a bow and arrow at point-blank range. Caravaggio's images freeze time but also seem to hover on the brink of their own disappearance. Faces are brightly illuminated. Details emerge from darkness with such uncanny clarity that they might be hallucinations. Yet always the shadows encroach, the pools of blackness that threaten to obliterate all. Looking at his pictures is like looking at the world by flashes of lightning. Caravaggio's life is like his art, a series of lightning flashes in the darkest of nights... Much of what is known about him has been discovered in the criminal archives of his time. The majority of his recorded acts – apart from those involved in painting – are crimes and misdemeanors." (3, p. 3)

Caravaggio was probably born in Milan. His father was in the service of a powerful noble family, the Sforza da Caravaggio, as a mason and majordomo. A young member of this noble family, the impetuous marchesa di Caravaggio would become the artist's hidden protector when he ran afoul of the law as he often would.

When the plague swept Milan in 1576, the Merisi family decamped to the town of Caravaggio which the artist would take as his name. Both his relatively well-off grandfather and his father died of the plague on the same day in 1577.

Caravaggio's mother was left a widow with four small children. Michelangelo went to school in Caravaggio and Rowland (4) suggests that because his family had been employed by nobility, he would have received a good classical education in a local grammar school. His brother, Giovanni Batista later attended a prestigious Jesuit College in Rome and became a priest.

Michelangelo, who had decided to become a painter, was apprenticed to a Milanese artist at 13 years of age. Langford suggests that Caravaggio may have already been involved in street crime and spent time in jail during his adolescent apprenticeship. (4)

His mother died in 1590, and Caravaggio took his inheritance and left for Rome, now the center of the Italian art-world. In the early 16th century, Rome was violent and dangerous, paralleling 16th century London where Shakespeare, Caravaggio's contemporary, was forced to tread lightly given the political and personal perils he faced as an immensely popular dramatist. For artists all across Europe these were uneasy times in the period of the Counter-Reformation particularly from political and ecclesiastic authorities if the artists' work was suspected of being subversive.

Initially, Caravaggio lived in bohemian circumstances in Rome selling his work on the streets. His talent soon brought him to the attention of Cardinal Francesco Del Monte, a wealthy and cultivated patron of the arts. He moved into Del Monte's opulent household and proceeded to paint a series of brilliant sensual paintings of male adolescents, including *The Lute Player* (now in the Hermitage Museum, St Petersburg) and *The Musicians* (now in the Metropolitan Museum of Art, New York). In the latter Caravaggio included himself in an early self-portrait, a practice he continued in many of his later paintings, making himself, the creator of the work, a central part of the action. Simultaneously, Caravaggio roamed the streets of Rome engaging in brawls, flaunting his sword which he was not supposed to wear and occasionally ending up in court as the police-blotter proves. His powerful patron, Del Monte, regularly bailed him out.

Under Del Monte's patronage his reputation soared and he obtained major church commissions, most notably for the Contarelli chapel of Chiesa Luigi dei Francesi. There Caravaggio created a remarkable cycle of paintings about the life of St Matthew in his revolutionary style where the viewer is drawn into the drama. He included a self-portrait (often used as the cover of biographies of the artist (3, 4)) which has a certain excruciating quality as he, the artist, vicariously watches the bloody execution of the saint, filled with pity and perhaps remorse.

After committing the murder of a local ward boss whom he killed in a dispute over a tennis match, he received a papal death sentence. This was serious and as Ingrid Rowland suggests: "Life was not so cheap after all in Baroque Rome." (4) He escaped (probably with the assistance of his powerful patrons) to Spanish-ruled Naples where he received and executed major commissions. He then journeyed to Malta where the Grand Master of the Knights of Saint John was eager to employ a great painter. In order to retain him, the grand master invested him as a knight. This required a papal dispensation since Caravaggio was a convicted murderer. It was not long before he found himself in prison, following a bloody brawl in which he was identified as the ringleader. Again, with the connivance of his patrons, he made a dramatic escape from prison and arrived in Sicily, where he continued to produce masterpieces. He then left for Naples where he was assaulted and his face severely slashed probably by pursuing agents of the Grand Master.

He recovered and knowing that Cardinal Scipione Borghese, the nephew of the Pope, was an admirer and collector of his work, he set out for Rome by ship in the hope of obtaining a papal pardon. He took with him recent paintings, including *David with the Head of Goliath*, where the severed head of Goliath is a self-portrait. Separated from his vessel by a misidentification and brief imprisonment at a port near Rome, he impulsively set out by foot along the coast where malaria was endemic to catch up to his boat with his paintings. He succumbed to malarial fever and died in a small hospital near the beach. His grave has never been found.

How to summarize Caravaggio's personality disorder and psychopathology? Early posthumous biographers of Caravaggio cite those who knew him personally as calling him "turbulent and quarrelsome", "a madman" and "dragged down by his own temperament." Easily aroused to volcanic rage, belligerent and violent in the extreme. Ultimately, I would suggest, profoundly masochistic in the sense of self-destructive. It is likely that he possessed some insight into this as his late painting *David with the Head of Goliath* (now in the Borghese Gallery, Rome) indicates, with Goliath as a frightening self-portrait. David, the precursor to Christ the Redeemer gates upon Goliath-Caravaggio with profound compassion, the absolution Caravaggio must have fervently desired.

REFERENCES

1) Pope-Hennessy, J: *The Piero Della Francesca Trail*. The Little Bookroom. New York, 2002.

2) Stone, DM: *Signature Killer: Caravaggio and the Poetics of Blood*. Art Bulletin, Dec 2012, Volume XCIV, Number 4, pp. 572-593.

3) Graham-Dixon, A: *Caravaggio: A Life Sacred & Profane*. WW Norton & Co. New York and London, 2012.

4) Langdon, H: *Caravaggio: A Life*. Farrar Straus and Giroux, New York 1998.

5) Fried, M: *The Moment of Caravaggio*. Princeton University Press. Princeton and Oxford, 2010.

JACKSON POLLOCK (1912–1956)

⚭

SUFFUSED BY ALCOHOL: THE RISE OF ABSTRACT EXPRESSIONISM

The eminent mid-20th century art critic, Clement Greenberg, is said to have referred to Jackson Pollock as "the most radical alcoholic I have ever known."

Alcoholism permeated the male practitioners of the abstract expressionist school which arose in New York City in the immediate post-World War II period when New York supplanted Paris as the epicenter of modern art. The male artists of the newly-emerging art movement, *action painting* as one critic called it, were all notorious drinkers. Before they became famous – as many of them eventually did – The Cedar Tavern in Greenwich Village was the site of their gatherings where arguments about the nature of formalist theory ("only the surface matters, content is irrelevant"), modern art in general and drunken brawls accompanying this 'discourse' were the order of the day.

Pollock was at the center of this scene before he moved to Eastern Long Island and his "drip" paintings championed by the afore-mentioned Clement Greenberg, catapulted him to a fame which has endured because of the originality and sheer beauty of many of these works. Painted on the floor by pouring paint on to the canvas, as Varnedoe observes in a catalogue of a retrospective of Pollock's work at the Museum of Modern Art in New York (1, 1998) … "The individual paintings of 1947-1950 were conceived in palettes that run from somber to gaudy, with surfaces that go from fudge to spun sugar, and in a range of emotional idioms – dark and light, snarled and nebular, aerated and choked, liquid and gritty" (1, p. 50). And further: "The drip paintings are far from uniformly successful. This way of working flirted with constant possible pitfalls, where assiduous color mixing could just yield mud, linear dynamism could get lost in splotchy, airless over-pouring, … and the desire for allover articulation could lead to fussiness or monotony." (1, p. 51) Pollock once asked his wife, the painter Lee Krasner, about a work in progress, not simply was it good or bad, but "is this a painting". (1, p. 51)

Pollock himself eloquently said: "My painting does not come from the easel. I hardly ever stretch my canvas before painting. I prefer to tack the unstretched canvas to the hard wall or to the floor. I need the resistance of a hard surface. On the floor I am more at ease. I feel nearer, more a part of the painting, since this way I can walk around it, work from the four sides and literally be in the painting. This is akin to the method of the Indian sand painters of the West.

"I continue to get farther away from the usual painter's tools such as easel palette, brushes etc. I prefer sticks, towels, knives and dripping fluid paint or a heavy impasto with sand, broken glass and other foreign material added.

"When I am in my painting, I'm not aware of what I am doing. It is only after a sort of "get acquainted" period that I see what I have been about. I have no fears about making changes, destroying the image etc. because the painting has a life of its own. I try to let it come through." (1, p. 48)

Varnedoe observes that Pollock's engagement with his highly original method of pouring paint on to the canvas on the floor, dancing around it from above as he administered almost-calligraphic lines and colors: "ruptured the existing definitions of how art could be made, and offered a new model of how one could be an artist. Spontaneity and chance ... were now brought forward into daylight as tools of concrete engagement with materials and the act of making, and submitted to a dialogue of control from which every tract didacticism and stock symbolism has been expunged." (1, p. 48)

Radical indeed, though this innovative approach has some antecedents in Japanese art both in pottery and calligraphy where spontaneity and 'accidents' in the act of creation were often valorized.

Pollock was born in Cody, Wyoming, the youngest of five sons. During his bohemian days in Greenwich Village he liked to refer to himself as 'the cowboy'. The Pollock family was peripatetic, roaming through Arizona, and Northern and Southern California, starting and leaving one failing business enterprise after another. According to Varnadoe: "Pollock's mother's vague but goading ambition to improve her circumstances made a bad match with the limited skills and ambitions of his father. That combination of hope and hopelessness kept the family on a restless trajectory... through a declining succession of ill-fated ventures in farming, fruit-growing, and managing a forlorn hotel." (1, p. 21) Varnedoe notes that Pollock's father became increasingly "depressive", a harbinger for what I would point out was Pollock's later affective disorder, manifest in violent mood swings, episodes of rage all exacerbated by his alcohol use.

Startlingly, three of the five sons became painters which must speak, in part, to the influence of their mother's esthetic interest. It was the eldest son Charles, who opened another world – that of

49

the artist – to Jackson. Pollock's first formal training in art began at sixteen in 1928 where he was enrolled at an art school in Los Angeles from which he was expelled, and then reinstated on two occasions for rebellious political activity.

At eighteen, he wrote a revealing *cri-de-cœur* to Charles: "I am continually having new experiences and am going through a wavering evolution which leave my mind in an unsettled state. … I have started doing some things with clay and have found a bit of encouragement from my teacher. My drawing I will tell you frankly is rotten. It seems to lack freedom and rhythm. It is cold and lifeless. … I think there should be an advancement soon. … the truth is I have never got down to real work and finish a piece. I usually get disgusted with it and lose interest. … although I feel I will make an artist of some kind I have never proven to myself nor anybody else that I have it in me. So called happy part of one's youth to me is a bit of damnable hell. If I could come to some conclusion about myself and life perhaps then I could see something to work for. My mind blazes up with some illusion for a couple of weeks then it smolders down to a bit of nothing. The more I read and the more I think I am nothing the darker things become…." (1, p. 22)

In 1930, Pollock joined Charles in New York and began studying at the Art Students League. His influential teacher was Thomas Hart Benton, a realist painter at the fore-front of the Regionalist movement painting everyday people across the United States. While at the Art Student League, Pollock became enamored of the Mexican mural movement personified by the artists Diego Rivera, Orozco and Siqueiros. In 1935, he started working for the Federal Arts Project. However, his emotional instability became apparent Charles recorded: "a complete loss of responsibility both to himself and to us. Accompanied by drinking." (1, p. 23)

In the late 1930s, Pollock entered what would turn out to be a sequence of psychotherapeutic treatments with one Jungian psychoanalyst after another. However, the most "therapeutic" influence that he encountered was meeting the talented painter Lee Krasner, who recognized his nascent talent, encouraged him and would ultimately become his wife. Artistically, Pollock was grappling with the titanic influence of Picasso and his deconstruction of the human body and the frame in his paintings. The masterpiece *Les Demoiselles d'Avignon* (1907) had recently been acquired by the Museum of Modern Art. Both this painting and Picasso's *Guernica* (depicting the horror of the saturation bombing of a Spanish Village by the German Condor Division during the Spanish civil war) also at that time in the Museum of Modern Art, had a profound influence on Pollock. (He is said to have expostulated *Defeat Picasso*.) He began to produce significant paintings such as *She-Wolf* (1943, now in the Museum of Modern Art). By now his palette was evolving to an "all-over" style with echoes of surrealism. He began to achieve significant recognition and had important gallery showings.

Still grappling with his inner demons and outbreaks of violent behavior, Krasner persuaded him to leave New York City, with its pernicious bar scene and settle with her in Eastern Long Island whose landscape with its ocean expanses appealed to him. Here, from 1947 to 1955, he created his greatest works. Krasner was also creating great abstract work herself during this period though it would only be recognized as such decades later. Their relationship as artists had a mutually beneficial, almost symbiotic nature.

Pollock's personal life continued to be fraught with tempestuous mood swings, alcoholic binges and violent outbursts. Krasner left for Europe in the summer of 1956. Two young female admirers visited Pollock in East Hampton. A drunken day led to his driving off the road near his studio, killing himself and one of the young women. A violent end to a violent and tortured life. Nonetheless, he is rightly regarded as one of the greatest painters of the 20th century because of the ground-breaking nature and beauty of the works of his maturity.

REFERENCES

1) Jackson Pollock: *Kirk Varnedoe with Pepe Karmel.* Published on the occasion of the exhibition Jackson Pollock Museum of Modern Art, New York. Nov 1, 1998 to Feb 2, 1999. Distributed by Harry N Abrams, Inc. New York, 1998.
2) Potter, J: *To a Violent Grave: An Oral Biography of Jackson Pollock.* G.P. Putnam's Sons. New York, 1985.

MARK ROTHKO (1903–1970)

∞

MAKING PEOPLE CRY

In his treatise, *the Trattato Della Pittura*, Leonardo Da Vinci (1452-1519) explained his views on the nature of art.

A famous passage in the *Trattato* states: "I shall not refrain from including among these precepts a new and speculative idea, which although it may seem trivial and almost laughable, is none less of great value in quickening the spirit of invention. It is this: that you should look at certain walls stained with damp or at stones of uneven color. If you have to invent some setting you will be able to see in these the likeness of divine landscapes." (1, p. 135)

Thus, did Mark Rothko create 'divine landscapes' in his abstract art. One of the greatest exponents of the mid-20th century abstract expressionist movement, he eschewed such a label and rejected the formalist doctrine that pervaded the art criticism of the period. "I'm not an abstractionist," Rothko stated. "I'm not interested in relationships of color or form or anything else. I'm interested only in expressing basic human emotions – tragedy, ecstasy, doom and so on – and the fact that lots of people break down and cry when confronted with my pictures shows that I communicate these basic human emotions."

Rothko's signature style that he developed in the late 1940's replaced imagery with color. As Waldman notes in her analysis of his painting entitled *Violet, Black, Orange, Yellow on White and Red* (1949, now in the Guggenheim Museum, New York): "He employs a series of horizontals within a vertical format and harmony is achieved by means of precise adjustment of a drastically reduced number of shapes and colors.... Rothko reveals one of the supreme features of his genius – his ability to hold on a single plane colors that advance and retreat" (2, pp. 56-57) As Messer perceptively observed: "Rothko shares with composers of music an absence of explicit imagery and a correspondingly developed capacity to evoke content by association – an interest in rhythmic structures and the use of color to achieve modulations that can be subtly chromatic or dramatically contrasted – he is a creator of melodic surfaces rendered vital and sonorous." (2, p. 12)

Born Marcus Rothkowitz in Dvinsk, Russia (now Latvia), Rothko was his parents' fourth child. His father, a pharmacist, immigrated alone to Portland, Oregon, in 1910. In 1913, the family was reunited, but Rothko's father died of colon cancer a year later. Rothko began sketching as a teenager and, an accomplished student, received a scholarship to attend Yale in 1921. When his scholarship was not renewed, he left the university and enrolled in the Art Students League in New York. The relationship he then developed with the painter Milton Avery was central to his artistic development. After a detour through surrealism he arrived at his signature style in the late 1940's and received wide recognition for his work. A thoughtful writer he stated: "I quarrel with surrealist and abstract art only as one quarrels with his father and mother, recognizing the inevitability and function of my roots, but insistent on my dissension: I, being both and an integral completely independent of them." (3, p. 178) This was a profound comment, acknowledging his artistic roots, yet asserting his independence and originality. In a lecture he gave in 1958, he declared that a meaningful work of art must have, first, a clear preoccupation with death and intimations of mortality and, second, sensuality, a lustful relationship with things that exist.

In New York City, Rothko became a member of a vibrant art scene that included Adolph Gottlieb, Barnett Newman and his mentor Milton Avery. He earned early recognition and was influenced by two important exhibitions at the Museum of Modern Art in 1936 – "Cubism and Abstract Art" and "Fantastic Art, Dada and Surrealism." Henri Matisse's *Red Studio* acquired by the Museum of Modern Art in 1949, was a work of both fascination and inspiration for Rothko. The abstract painter Clifford Still was another important influence on Rothko as well as a friend.

Rothko's first marriage ended in divorce and he had two children by his second wife. His biographer Breslin recounts an episode from the late 1940s which speaks to Rothko's emotional vicissitudes (this occurred shortly after the death of his mother): "Spending the summer in East Hampton, Rothko embarked on an ill-fated fishing trip off the Long Island shore… with Harold Rosenberg and Jackson Pollock… The boat was leaky, it began to take on water and eventually to sink. The three other men jumped and swam for shore, but Rothko, though a strong swimmer, hung onto the side of the sinking boat until the last possible moment, then swam in. When Lee Krasner, who had been sitting with Clement Greenberg on the beach asked Rothko what had happened, he said that "as the boat went down, and he stayed there unable to plunge into the water and start swimming, he was thinking of his mother." (3, p. 266)

Rothko separated from his second wife in 1969, a year prior to his suicide. By then he had achieved considerable fame, epitomized by the commission for The Rothko Chapel by the de Menil family in Houston, Texas. This was, and became, a place of pilgrimage focused on the spirituality of Rothko's paintings. He was never to see its fruition.

In the late 1960s, Rothko was treated for depression. He had been diagnosed as having an aortic aneurysm. Surgical intervention was ruled out because of liver disease, a consequence of years of heavy drinking.

In 1970, he killed himself in his studio by severing both brachial arteries with a razor blade. Just prior he created a series of *Black on Gray* paintings. Breslin notes: "The *Black on Gray* paintings are not simply avant-garde efforts to thwart the expectations of an art market perfectly capable of absorbing any and all gestures of resistance. They are not mere formalist experiments, designed to test how much Rothko could subtract and still have a painting… As distanced and controlled as they are, the *Black on Gray* paintings are still strongly emotional: they quite openly express the urge to withdraw, to retreat, 'rock shut as a seashell'. It is not just that these paintings comment on Rothko's death: his suicide commented on these paintings: these feelings, Rothko was asserting, are real." (3, p. 530)

Rothko viewed his paintings as a "portal" into profound emotional states. In his mature work he embodies for the viewer one aspect of Rudolph Otto's concept of numinous, the *mysterium fascinans*, the capacity to attract, fascinate and compel.

REFERENCES

1) Clark, K: *Leonardo da Vinci*, Penguin Books, London, 1988.

2) Waldman, D: *Mark Rothko, 1903-1970, A Retrospective*, The Salomon R. Guggenheim Museum, New York. Harry N. Abrams, Inc., New York, 1978.

3) Breslin, James EB: *Mark Rothko: A Biography*, The University of Chicago Press, Chicago and London, 1993.

TRAUMA: INTRODUCTION

၁ာ

The three painters discussed in this section all suffered from traumatic experiences which they later expressed in their artistic creations.

Trauma is common in everyday life. It can take many forms, from the unexpected loss of a loved one to a serious motor vehicle accident, the diagnosis of a life-threatening illness, or being the victim of an assault. Nearly all people have an immediate stress response disorder to acute trauma, expressed in feelings of helplessness, horror, fear or anger. Most recover rapidly, but a small percentage will go on to develop persistent post-traumatic stress disorder.

Nancy Andreasen, whose original study of creativity and mental illness was the progenitor of this book (see introduction), observed that burn patients universally experienced an acute stress disorder subsequent to their injuries and some went on to develop persistent PTSD. Her work led to the establishment of PTSD in the official DSM-III nomenclature in 1980. (1, 2)

Francisco Goya (1746-1828), the radical Spanish artist who declared: "There are no rules in painting" portrayed in his series of etchings *The Disasters of War* a devastating depiction of the traumatic horrors that resulted from Napoleon's invasion of Spain. Goya himself had a traumatic experience when in 1792 he contracted a serious illness marked by episodes of syncope, severe tinnitus, semi blindness, and disturbances of balance. Some speculate that this was meningitis, for upon his recovery he was completely deaf. Shortly thereafter he painted two of his grimmest paintings, *The Madhouse* and *Interior of a Prison*. One could speculate that these remarkable visceral paintings were a 'therapeutic' expression of his traumatic experience.

Descriptions, both personal and clinical of PTSD have existed for centuries. Classic examples include accounts of the psychological consequences of frightening combat situations. Some soldiers who engaged in the murderous trench warfare of World War I, in which combatants were slaughtered in droves, developed dissociative flashbacks of terrifying combat experiences when they were no longer at the front-line. These were combined with recurrent nightmares in which the life-threatening experiences would be repeated over and over again. The same phenomenon was seen during World War II, the Korean war and the Vietnam conflict and has been a persistent element for some combatants in the contemporary military engagements in Iraq, Afghanistan and elsewhere.

The British writer, Pat Barker, in her *Regeneration* trilogy (3) has provided the most compelling literary expression of this syndrome and its attempted treatment at the hands of the real-life anthropologist-psychiatrist W.H.R. Rivers (1864-1922). Rivers is a remarkable figure in both the history of psychiatry and cultural anthropology to which he made many important contributions. (4) Influenced by Freud's theories, he employed a 'cathartic' psychological therapy to treat the 'shell-shock' of World War I veterans. His patients included the writers Siegfried Sassoon and Robert Graves. (The latter wrote a bitter account of his war-time experience and his subsequent traumatic disorder in his powerful memoir, *Goodbye to All That*.) (5)

60

Rivers' 'cathartic' treatment method was far from successful, echoing the equivocal results for 'exposure' therapy for PTSD today.

What may be useful in mitigating the persistent, dysphoric memory of past trauma may be, if the sufferer has the capacity, the expression of the experience in writing (the plethora of contemporary published accounts in the recent literature of varying traumatic experiences from being abused as a child to serving in Iraq would suggest this may be so) to, in the case of the three artists in this section, visual expression through painting.

REFERENCES

1) Andreasen, NC, Moyes, R Jr., Hartford, CE et al: *Management of Emotional reactions in seriously burned adults.* N Engl J Med 286: 65-69, 1912

2) American Psychiatric Association: *Diagnostic and Statistical Manual of Mental Disorders*, 3rd Edition, Washington DC, American Psychiatric Association, 1980.

3) Barker, P: *The Regeneration Triology*, Viking Press, New York, 1991.

4) Slobodin, R; *W.H.R. Rivers*, Colombia University Press, New York, 1978.

5) Graves, R: *Goodbye to All That.* Anchor Press, New York, 1958 (2nd Edition).

ALBRECHT DÜRER (1471-1528)

∾

SELF-REFLECTION AND MELANCHOLIA

Albrecht Dürer's great engraving *Melencolia* (1514) is a haunting work that speaks to mortality, morbid introspection, the baleful influence of Saturn, and, as announced on the left-hand side, depression, i.e. melancholia, accompanied by a flaming comet.

Interpretation of this remarkable work have been manifold. The art-historian Mitchell Merback has devoted a monograph to the image and called it: "one of the most talked about pictures of the European canon, a portrait of creative endeavor poised between inspired breakthrough and demoralizing breakdown." (1, p. 10) Further, he comments: "the total atmosphere, with its weird airlessness and incantatory power, its surreal assemblage of unlike things, seems to evoke the kind of delusions to which physicians and churchmen (of the time) thought morbid melancholics acutely susceptible." (1, p. 16) Merback further asserts that: "*Melencolia*'s challenge to the beholder ... takes on the quality of restoring and fostering health." (1, p. 18) That is, in his opinion, it has a potentially therapeutic function for the beholder.

Significantly, this masterwork was created shortly after Dürer's mother's death. As Dürer noted in his *Book of Remembrances*, "She feared death very much... Also she died hard... I have such sorrow from this that I cannot express it." (1, p. 178) But express it he did in his great engraving. In my opinion *Melencolia* is a work of grief and mourning, for the death of his mother.

Dürer's great contemporary, Matthias Grünewald, about whom little is known, painted the *Isenheim Altarpiece* between 1512 and 1516. It now resides in Colmar in Alsace, France, and is generally regarded as one of the supreme masterpieces of the Northern Renaissance.

The work was originally installed in what was essentially a hospital, the monastic establishment of the Canons Regular of Saint Anthony which tended to patients who were mortally ill with St Anthony's fire, a type of ergot poisoning that resulted from eating infected grain. The painting was intended to be psychologically therapeutic and provide comfort and succor to the patients in the hospital through communion and identification with the depiction of the crucified Christ and the vision of subsequent transcendence. Thus it bears resemblance to Merback's thesis of the 'therapeutic' implications of Dürer's *Melencolia*.

As Smith comments: "For Grünewald, Christ was a physical model and spiritual balm ... the focus is on his body with its rippled flesh pricked with thorns, its congealed streams of blood and its grotesque distortion." The sufferers of St Anthony's fire suffered similar torments with ravaged blackened limbs whose feet and hands developed gangrene. In one of the side-panels of the altarpiece there is a pustule-covered demon who exhibits symptoms of the disease. Smith notes: "The despondent mood and dark tonalities of the exterior are swept away once the altarpiece is opened to its middle setting ... In the Resurrection one of the most majestic figures in the history of art, slowly rises from his tomb ... embodies hope to the hospital's sick, their physical suffering, like his, would pass. Death was a release, hopefully, to a better place." (2, p. 221) Hence, the 'therapeutic' potential of art was definitely in the air, as expressed by both Grünewald and Dürer in their masterworks.

Dürer's father was of Hungarian origin and left his home village for Burgundy where he could receive the best possible training as a goldsmith. He then settled in Nuremburg, a city of international importance in both trade and culture. There he married the daughter of a well-to-do goldsmith and established a successful practice.

Between 1468 and 1492, eighteen children were born to the couple, only three of whom survived into childhood Albrecht Dürer was the eldest to survive. Hutchinson, a biographer of Dürer suggested that he "can scarcely have failed to be affected by the deaths of so many of his brothers and sisters – saddened of course, yet perhaps acquiring something of the sense of his own uniqueness and importance." (3, p. 20) This sense of his own 'uniqueness and importance' was to find expression in the remarkable self-portraits that he created during his artistic career.

Four years before his death Dürer wrote a history of his family. He observes: "And my father took special interest in me because he saw that I was diligent in striving to learn. So he sent me to the school and when I had learned to read and write he took me away from it and taught me the goldsmith's craft. But when I could work neatly, my liking drew me more to painting than to goldsmith's work. So I put it to my father. But he was troubled, for he regretted the time lost while I had been learning to be a goldsmith. Still he let me have my way." (3, p. 20)

Thus, against his better judgement Dürer's father apprenticed his son, already an accomplished craftsman, to a local painter who was also renowned for his mastery of wood-cuts. Early on, Dürer became a master. His woodcuts, etchings and engravings, redolent with evocative imagery and widely distributed throughout late-Renaissance Europe in multiple copies became enormously popular. In his use of multiple copies of the same powerful image and their rapid distribution he anticipated Andy Warhol and his 'factory' of multiple silk-screened prints in 20th century New York.

Dürer achieved extraordinary mastery of silver-point engraving reflected in his first self-portrait in this medium at the age of thirteen. As Smith comments on the 1504 engraving *Adam and Eve*: "The believable three-dimensionality of *Adam & Eve* is achieved by a profound understanding of anatomy, by the play of lights and shadows dancing across their bodies and by the absolute mastery of the engraved line ... with its emphasis on human beauty rather than mortal sin it caused a sensation." (2, pp. 265-266)

In the summer of 1494, Butterfield notes that: "Soon after his engagement Dürer made a strangely intimate drawing of his fiancée Agnes Frey, now in the Albertina, Vienna. One might have expected a 23-year-old to depict his betrothed as a source of love, or comfort, or well-being ... Instead Albrecht showed Agnes twisted up in a knot of anxious introversion ... there had never been a drawing quite like this ... Dürer was fascinated by the close scrutiny of dark and brooding emotion." (4) It was to be a childless, perhaps unromantic but nevertheless constant marriage. Shortly after his wedding Dürer left alone for Italy for an extended stay. Around this time, he developed an intimate and enduring friendship with Willibald Pirckheimer, one of Germany's leading humanists and a correspondent of the eminent philosopher Erasmus. Pirckheimer recognized Dürer's genius and financially underwrote his second journey to Italy where the Venetian painter Giovanni Bellini sang Dürer's praises. Like da Vinci, Dürer's interest in the natural world was immense. He created the first printed celestial chart and his beautifully rendered drawings and painting of animals, birds and plants have never been surpassed.

By 1520, Dürer had ascended to international fame and was a member of the Nuremburg delegation to the coronation of the Holy Roman Emperor, Charles V. As Hutchinson notes, he had become at that time "in the strictest sense of the term, the most celebrated artist who ever lived." (3, p. 187)

On Dürer's death, Martin Luther wrote: "It is natural and right to weep for so excellent a man." (3, p. 184)

Dürer was the first artist to leave a series of self-portraits. One now in Munich's Alte Pinakothek (1500) is clearly an image of himself embodying Christ. As a portrait it bears comparison with Leonardo's *Mona Lisa* (1503) in its powerful intensity and capacity to totally engage the viewer in an almost hypnotic experience in which one is drawn into a type of visual communion.

In his graphite drawing self-portrait in the nude (1508) Dürer daringly embraces an unflinching raw physicality that would not find further such expression until the 20th century in the work of the British artist Lucien Freud.

Significantly, Dürer's self-portrait as a melancholic (1516) seems to speak to his life-long emotional disposition. I would suggest that this is one that arose him from his childhood experiences constantly summoned by the premature death of siblings, reinforced by the death of his beloved mother and that found artistic expression in his great engraving *Melencolia*.

REFERENCES

1) Merback, MB: *Perfection's Therapy. An Essay on Albrecht Dürer's Melancholia 1*. Zone Books, New York, 2017.

2) Smith, JC: *The Northern Renaissance*, Phaidon Press, New York, 2004.

3) Hutchinson, JC: *Albrect Dürer A Biography*. Princeton University Press, Princeton, New Jersey, 1990.

4) Butterfield, A: *Review of Albrecht Dürer: Master Drawings, Watercolors and Prints from the Albertina*. National Gallery of Art, Washington DC, The New York Review of Books, May 20, 2003.

ARTEMESIA GENTILESCHI
(1593–1653)

∽☙∽

REVENGE AND RECOGNITION

As Mary Gabriel relates in the introduction to her seminal book, *Ninth Street Women: Lee Krasner, Elaine de Kooning, Grace Hartigan, Joan Mitchell and Helen Frankenthaler. Five Painters and the Movement That Changed Modern Art*: "The idea for this book arose out of a conversation I had with painter Grace Hartigan, in the fall of 1990. At sixty-eight, she was in the midst of her biggest year in decades with multiple exhibitions scheduled and a monograph of her work newly released ... I was in the presence of a woman who had sacrificed everything, including her only child, to be what she was: an artist," (1, p. xi)

As Gabriel observes: "Grace was part of the art movement born in the 1930s that shifted the capital of Western culture from Paris to New York and changed the very history of art." (1, p. xii)

In a trenchant review of Gabriel's book, Claudia Roth Pierpont (2) chronicles the vicissitudes and triumphs of the careers of these enormously talented and fiercely determined women artists who were constantly running up against the rampant misogyny of mid-20th century America where men, and male artists dominated.

With the passage of time, their genius has been recognized and they have ascended to the pantheon of the greatest modern artists. It is telling of the times in which they worked that Helen Frankenthaler, who invented a technical breakthrough in abstract art by applying diluted paint to her canvasses – a stain technique – was not recognized as the innovator of this radical method of abstract painting. Male artists who adopted it were given the critical accolades for its implementation in their work.

Significant women painters able to pursue a professional career, earn a living from their vocation, and receive public recognition, barely existed until the late 19th century.

A rare exception was Artemisia Gentileschi, generally recognized as one of the great painters of the Italian Baroque period. As Harris noted: "Artemisia Gentileschi is the first woman in the history of Western art to make a significant and undeniably important contribution to the art of her time." (3, pp. 118-119)

In her work, Artemisia, like her father Orazio, embraced the radical naturalistic tradition initiated by Caravaggio, which, as Christiansen observed, she took to a new level: "the brush is handled with great looseness. The surface effects—achieved by a constant layering and blending of lights and darks—are incomparably richer and the harsh focused illumination of Caravaggio is exchanged for the haunting effects of candlelight used less to freeze the action within the confines of the canvas than to animate it and suggest an expansion of space beyond the frame of the picture." (4, p. 107)

The magnitude of her artistic achievement has sometimes been obscured by historical preoccupations with lurid and sensational aspects of her early life history. These include posing for her father as a nude life model; her rape by one of his studio assistants, Agostino

Tassi, when she was 17; and the subsequent trial of Tassi, during which her testimony was given while strings were tightened around her fingers. This torture was considered mild and ostensibly was administered to ensure the veracity of her deposition. Shortly after her trial (the rapist was convicted), Artemisia married and decamped from Rome to Florence. There she gave birth to four children, and her career, freed from the shadow of her father and his atelier, flourished under the patronage of the Medici court. Christiansen observes: "It is in Florence that Artemisia's status as an independent artist really begins … she established bonds of friendship with the leading Florentine painter Cristofano Allori, the court poet and playwright Michelangelo Buonarroti the younger, and Galileo." (4, p. 114)

Artemisia was the oldest of four children. Her mother died when she was 10. She began her apprenticeship in her father's studio as a teenager. Her father was an established but middling painter until his work was transformed by his encounter with Caravaggio in 1600. Christiansen asserts that "this was the central event of his life – the work of Caravaggio demanded a rethinking of the relationship between artist and model, the imagined and the real, the painter and his artifact. In the critical language of the day it opposed truth, or il vero to verisimilitude (verosimile) by which ordinary experience was transposed into the exemplary and ideal." (5, p. 5)

Orazio went on to achieve considerable renown as a Caravaggist, and he was appointed a court painter to King Charles the 1st of England.

By 1610, at the age of 17, Artemisia had created the stunning painting *Susanna and the Elders* in which a beautiful maiden is spied on in her bath by two lascivious old men (now in Moravská Galerie, Brno). Some have suggested that this painting had autobiographical meaning for Artemisia and that the two elders represent Orazio and her rapist Tassi. Christiansen commented that in Artemisia's paintings: "we ought not to underrate the role of anger in [her] work – not simply against Tassi – but against her father and the circumstances of her life, both private and professional." (4, p. 111) Her remarkable *Judith and the Holofernes* (now in the Museo Nazionale di Capodimonte, Naples) speaks to this issue. As recounted in the Book of Judith, Holofernes was an Assyrian general who launched an invasion of Israel and was poised to destroy Judith's home city. A famous beauty, Judith gained access to his camp, gained his trust and aroused his desire. While courting her in his tent, he became intoxicated and passed out, and Judith decapitated him, thus saving her homeland. Ultimately, Artemisia can be celebrated as a great female artist who surmounted trauma on many fronts and achieved revenge and resolution through the application and recognition of her artistic genius.

REFERENCES

1) Gabriel, M: *Ninth Street Women*. Little, Brown and Company. New York, Boston, London, 2018.

2) Piermont, CR: *How New York's Postwar Female Painters Battled for Recognition*. The New Yorker, Oct 1st, 2018.

3) Harris, AS: *Nochlin: Women Artists, 1550-1950*. Knopf, New York, 1977.

4) Christiansen, K: *Becoming Artemisia: After-Thoughts on the Gentileschi Exhibition*. Metropolitan Museum Journal 2004, 39: 101-126.

5) Christiansen, K: *The Art of Orazio Gentileschi*, in Orazio and Artemisia Gentileschi. Edited by Christiansen, K., Mann, J.W., New York, Metropolitan Museum of Art, New York, 2001, pp. 2-8.

FRIDA KAHLO (1907-1954)

∽∞∾

TRAUMA, PAIN, THE BODY AND DEFIANCE

Frida Kahlo is an inspirational figure in the history of modern art. Her traumatic, romantically tempestuous and illness-scarred life found manifestation and expression in her remarkable paintings. Within her haunting work and especially her self-portraits, she expressed the theme of a woman triumphant in the face of both physical and psychic trauma, valorized the vibrant indigenous culture of Mexico, and gave a powerful visual life to the plight of the impoverished and down-trodden in her native country.

In some ways she was an heir to Goya (1756-1828), who was also unrelenting in his unvarnished portrayals of social and political iniquities. It is also no accident that she was enamored of the 16th century Flemish painters, Hieronymus Bosch and Pieter Bruegel, who, in their sometimes phantasmagoric canvases, expressed the horrors of unbridled and brutal human behavior that occurred in the prolonged war (1568-1648), when the Spanish engaged in a scorched-earth attempt to suppress the independence movement within Flanders and Holland. (1, p. 276)

Kahlo was the third of four daughters. She was born in a house in Mexico City (now a national museum) built by her parents. It was where she was ultimately to die. Her father Wilhelm was an immigrant from Germany. He pursued a successful career in Mexico as a professional photographer. At one point he was commissioned by the Mexican government to compile a photographic record of architectural monuments of the pre-Columbian and colonial periods. Kahlo was entranced by her father who taught her how to use a camera, an experience which may have contributed to her becoming an artist. When she contracted polio at the age of six, which left her with a withered left leg, her father took assiduous care of her. A lyrical painting from 1951, created in the last years of her life: *Portrait of My Father* (Frida Kahlo Museum, Mexico City) captures her loving and admiring feelings toward him.

Her feelings about her Mexican mother were more ambivalent, though she came to embrace a Mexican identity and often wore the colorful peasant dresses and shawls of Mexican Indian women. She recounted to the art critic Raquel Tibol: "My mother was unable to breast-feed me because my sister Cristina was born just eleven months after I was. I was fed by a wet nurse… In one of my pictures I show myself, with the face of a grown woman and the body of a little girl, in the arms of my nurse, milk dripping from breasts as from the heavens." (2, p. 8) The painting is *My Nurse and I or Me Suckling* (Museo Dolores Olmedo, Mexico City).

In 1925, at the age of 18, Kahlo sustained multiple serious injuries when a streetcar crashed into the bus she was riding. Her ribs, pelvis, and spinal column were fractured and a hand-rail from the streetcar penetrated her back and emerged through her vagina. During her prolonged convalescence, she was confined in casts and spent her time in her childhood bed which had a canopy with a full-length mirror. She constantly contemplated her broken body. It was then that she began to paint "as a means of escaping the boredom and pain." (2, p. 17) Prior to this catastrophic accident she had planned to become a physician. However, regarding her convalescence, Frida recounted, "I felt I still had enough energy to do something other than studying to become a doctor. Without giving it any particular thought, I started painting." (2, p. 17)

During this bed-ridden convalescence, undoubtedly inspired by viewing herself in the mirror over her bed, she began a series of self-portraits which were ultimately to comprise some thirty-percent of her total *œuvre*. She explained this concentration on self-portraits by declaiming: "I paint self-portraits because I am so often alone, because I am the person I know best." (2, p. 14)

By 1927, she had recovered somewhat, was ambulatory, and met the already-famous Mexican muralist Diego Rivera. He encouraged her artistic career. In 1929, they married. This was destined to be a tumultuous, tempestuous relationship scarred by multiple infidelities on both sides, with divorce and re-marriage. During their first marriage, Rivera had an affair with Kahlo's sister, Cristina. Kahlo was not simply the passive victim of Rivera's womanizing, she had numerous affairs herself including with Leon Trotsky, whom both she and Rivera had sponsored for asylum and residence in Mexico after he was expelled from the Soviet Union by Stalin. Following his assassination by a Soviet agent, Kahlo was investigated by Mexican security forces because she was acquainted with the murderer. She was cleared of any involvement.

Her life-long passion for Rivera, however, is captured in her classic self-portrait wherein he appears as a painted icon on her forehead. (Collection, Jaques and Natalia Gelman, Mexico City)

In an entry in her diary she writes: "Every moment, he is my child. My newborn babe, every little while, every day of my own self." (1, p. 205)

Both Kahlo and Rivera embraced communism, but when Rivera was expelled from the Party in 1929, she also resigned. In 1930, the couple moved to the United States where Rivera had been offered numerous commissions. The most notorious was that in Rockefeller Center in New York City, commissioned by the Rockefeller family. This nearly-completed mural was obliterated when Rivera refused to remove the prominent portrait of Lenin in the painting.

While in Detroit, where Rivera worked on another commission, Kahlo's second pregnancy (the first had been terminated) ended in a miscarriage. This traumatic experience was to find expression in her graphic painting of 1932: *Henry Ford Hospital or the Flying Bed* (Museo Dolores Olmedo, Mexico City). In this painting, the artist lies in a pool of blood in a hospital bed surrounded by images of the dead fetus, a pelvis, a wilted flower, all connected by cords to her body. Another startling painting from 1932 entitled *My Birth* (private collection) visualizes the artist's view of her own birth where the head of the mother is covered by a shroud.

As the writer Carlos Fuentes in an introduction to the publication of Kahlo's diary wrote: "The horrible, the painful can lead us to a path of self-knowledge. It then becomes beautiful simply because it identifies our very beings, our innermost qualities. Kahlos's self-portraits are beautiful for the same reason as Rembrandt's. They show us the successive identities of a human being who is not yet, but who is becoming." (1, p. 16) Further Fuentes writes "Kahlo was more like a broken Cleopatra, hiding her tortured body, her shriveled leg, her broken foot, her orthopedic corsets, under the spectacular finery of the peasant women of Mexico ... The laces, the ribbons, the skirts, the rustling petticoats, the braids, the moonlike headdresses, opening up her face like the wings of a dark butterfly. Frida Kahlo showing us all that suffering could not wither, nor sickness stale, her infinite variety." (1, p. 8)

Lowe notes in her essay accompanying the publication of Kahlo's diary: "In the self-portraits, Kahlo painted with fore-thought. She carefully constructs herself in a variety of settings, creating an artistic persona with an audience in mind. The paintings are provocative and aggressively audacious both in subject matter and in intent. Before Kahlo, Western art was unused to images of birthing or miscarriage, double self-portraits with visible internal organs or cross-dressing, as subjects for 'high art.'" (1, p. 25)

In 1950, Kahlo's health continued to decline. Her right leg was amputated because of gangrene in 1953. She died in 1954. Cremated, her ashes were placed in a pre-Columbian vase in her childhood home La Casa Azul.

I would suggest that Kahlo used her art to powerful effective therapeutic effect, as a means of treating and mitigating the debilitating psychological effect of multiple physical and psychic traumas that she experienced thus creating a radical body of great art.

As a final assertion of her indomitable, creative and rebellious spirit, right before she died, across her last painting she wrote: *Viva La Vida.*

REFERENCES

1) *Kahlo.* Andrea Kettenmann. Taschen, 2015, Köln, Germany.

2) *The Diary of Frida Kahlo.* Abrams, New York, 2005.

DISORDERS OF SELF: INTRODUCTION

⤷⤸

The psychiatric delineation of personality disorders began in the 19th century. Psychiatric attention focused initially on the psychology and behavior of the so-called "criminal personality." Hence "anti-social personality disorder" – in common parlance the "psychopath" – was the first of the personality disorders to be described. (1)

While most psychiatric syndromes are viewed in terms of presenting psychopathology, "borderline personality disorder" was "discovered in the office of the psycho-dynamically-oriented psychotherapist. The concept is clinically derived. It was first recognized because these patients became worse when treated with intensive psychotherapy and revealed far more serious psychopathology than was suspected at the initial evaluation. They were viewed as more well-integrated "neurotic" individuals at assessment but manifested impulsive, self-destructive and demanding behaviors when intensive psychotherapeutic treatment was initiated. The transference rapidly became intense, filled with anger or with inappropriate expressions of "love" or intense erotic feelings. Often extreme idealization of the therapist alternated with massive devaluation. Hence in the consulting room with the borderline patient, one is in the realm of the wildly unpredictable interactive, echoing what the viewer may experience, in muted form, in confronting great works of art (*cf.* "The Stendhal Syndrome").

Personality disorders represent a syndrome that encompasses cognition, affectivity, interpersonal functioning, behavior, coping and ego defenses. They are often mixed in nature. For instance, narcissistic personality disorder is a relatively recent diagnostic category. Narcissistic patients were often viewed by the world as high-functioning and without obvious psychopathology. They suffered, although they often denied it, and only their therapists realized its depth. It seemed from the beginning that narcissism was more of a theme in mental life than a distinct nosological category. It was essentially universal, although more prominent in some than in others and it could be associated with a wide range of pathology, from relatively healthy to seriously disturbed.

The five artists described in this section, all exhibited personality disorders. Cézanne was hypersensitive, easily insulted and irascible. However his suspicious view of the world may have been critical to his innovative painting. Cornell's obsession with his imaginary world is apparent. Courbet's identity was that of an extravagant personage who declared: "when I am dead let this be said of me – he belonged to no school, no church, to no institution, to no academy, least of all to any regime except the regime of liberty." And one could add adherence to the regime of original self-regard. Gauguin prided himself on his transformation from "civilized European" to "Savage Savant" but it was clearly not an easy shift.

REFERENCE

MacKinnon, RA, Michels R, Buckley PJ: *The Psychiatric Interview in Clinical Practice*, 3rd Edition, American Psychiatric Publishing, 2016

PAUL CÉZANNE (1839–1906)

⌒⌒

SEEING THE WORLD DIFFERENTLY
AND WITH SUSPICION

Because of the radical and transformative nature of his paintings, Paul Cézanne has garnered the attention (and adoration) of poets, philosophers, art-critics, and the public. Essentially unrecognized in his lifetime (except by fellow artists such as Monet) he achieved enduring fame only at the end of his life.

"For one thinks of him as a prophet," the poet Rainer Maria Rilke wrote in 1916. (1, p. ix) "Today I went to see his pictures again; it's remarkable what a surrounding they create ... one feels their presence drawing together into a colossal reality. As if these colors could heal one of indecision once and for all ... you get the impression that they are doing something for you." (1, pp. 45-46) "... no-one before him ever demonstrated so clearly the extent to which painting is something that takes place among the colors, and how one has to leave them completely alone so that they can come to terms among themselves. Their mutual intercourse: this is the whole of painting." (1, p. 66)

Maurice Merleau-Ponty, the 20th Century French philosopher wrote: "We live in the midst of man-made objects, among tools, in houses, streets, cities and most of the time we see them only through the human actions which put them to use. We become used to thinking that all of this exists necessarily and unshakably Cézanne's painting suspends these habits of thought and reveals the base of inhuman nature upon which man has installed himself." (2, p. 16)

As the art-critic John Russell observed: Cézanne "rebuilt the experience of seeing. He rebuilt it on the canvas, touch by touch … it had to be true to the object seen … it had to be true to the experience of seeing." In essence, Cézanne was "reconstructing the act of cognition." (3, p. 31)

Through this leap of the imagination and its realization on canvas, Cézanne, alongside Manet, became the progenitor of Modernism, wherein the language of painting shifted radically in form and content and was no longer concerned with imitating nature.

Picasso asserted "Cézanne is the father of us all." Early in his career, when he could ill-afford it, Matisse bought a small painting by Cézanne which he kept in his studio throughout his creative life. A virtual icon, it was a constant inspiration. Both Picasso and Matisse, separately and distinctively, built on Cézanne's reconstruction of what we actually 'see' and proceeded to extend his vision.

Cézanne was born in Aix-en-Provence, France, out of wedlock. Subsequently, his father married his mother and two more children, both girls, were born. Cézanne's father became a highly successful banker in Aix, but experienced social rejection in the class-conscious society of the provincial town because of his 'lowly' origins. Renald notes: "The kind of ostracism to which his family was subjected left its mark on Paul, who was proud and sensitive and accentuated his introspective tendencies. Later when he reached manhood, Cézanne avoided society and found it very difficult to make friends." (4, p. 21)

Cézanne's father wanted his son to become a lawyer and join the bank. It was only with great reluctance that he subsidized his son's determination not to do so and pursue a career as a painter. (After his father's death, Cézanne stated: "My father was a man of genius; he left me an income of 25,000 francs." (4, p. 123)

During his school days in Aix, Cézanne became best friends with Émile Zola. Cézanne was older than Zola and protected him from school-yard bullying. Zola was to attain renown in his own right as a journalist, novelist, art-critic and polemicist, most notably for his essay *J'accuse* which attacked the flagrantly anti-Semitic Dreyfus trial (1894) with its fabricated charges of treason against a Jewish army officer.

Throughout adolescence and into adulthood, Cézanne and Zola were mutual intellectual catalysts and soul mates.

Cézanne's biographer Dancher asserts that: "Cézanne's relationship with Zola was the main axis of his emotional life from cradle to grave. Theirs was one of the seminal artistic liaisons … Their feeling for each other was anchored in shared experience as artist-creators against the grain." (5, p. 29)

Dancher notes: "[Zola's] early writing fairly pulsates with contempt for the good for nothing bourgeois … The last line of *Le Ventre de Paris* (1873) is the Cézanne's characters parting shot – one of the real Cézanne's favorite expressions – a muttered imprecation against the plump of the world: "What bastards respectable people are." (5, p. 18)

By 1861, both Cézanne and Zola were living in Paris pursuing their careers as self-proclaimed radical artists. Zola was living in straightened circumstances; Cézanne was better off thanks to the annuity he received from his father.

During this period, Zola was already observing Cézanne's volatile moods: "Such a character and such impulsive and unreasonable changes of behavior … If by chance he advances a contrary opinion and you dispute it, he flies into a rage without wishing to examine, screams that you know nothing about the subject." (5, pp. 30-31)

Their friendship did not survive the publication of Zola's novel *L'Oeuvre* (1886) (The Masterpiece) with its depiction of the thwarted artistic quest personified by his intimate friend. Cézanne had a violent reaction to the thinly disguised and derogatory portrait that Zola 'painted' of him. He may have been incensed by one line in the novel: "Did one ever know in art where madness began?"

In 1863 Cézanne began a working relationship with the impressionist painter Camille Pissaro, painting together in the countryside and environs of Paris. Pissaro early on recognized his talent, comparing him to the great Renaissance Venetian painter Veronese. This was a revolutionary time in French art. Manet's *Le Dejeuner Sur L'hérbe* appeared at this time. This painting aroused public and critical indignation with its portrayal of a nude woman in the company of men who are wearing clothes, even though such a content had many classical antecedents, such as Titian and Giorgione. Rewald notes that if Cézanne "learned anything from Manet, it was doubtless how to organize space in definite planes." (4, p. 48)

Cézanne's romantic life was fraught. Renoir recalled that Cézanne commented: "I paint still-lifes. Women models frighten me. The sluts are always watching to catch you off your guard." (6, p. 30) This was an expression of his life-long suspicion of other people's motives.

In 1869, Cézanne returned to Paris from Aix and fell in love with a young model, Hortense Fiquet, some eleven years younger. With her he had a son out of wedlock, thus replicating his father's behavior and his own experience. While this marriage was unhappy, Cézanne was an indulgent and affectionate father who maintained a happy relationship with his son throughout his life.

Ultimately, Cézanne returned to Aix where the environs were his abiding creative and emotional center as his late great paintings of Monte Sainte-Victoire attest. "But when one is born down there, it is no use, nothing else seems to mean anything." (4, p. 239)

In 1890 he wrote: "Isolation is what I am worthy of. Thus, at least, no one gets me in his clutches." (4, p. 185) The same year, he also commented "All artists, parbleu, more or less always go a bit off the rails, this way or that ... You have to be incorruptible in your art, and to be so in your art, you have to train yourself to be so in your life." (5, p. 27)

In 1895, Monet who was famous and revered hosted a small party at his home in Giverny for Cézanne. Monet gave a brief speech: "At last we are all here together and happy to seize the occasion to tell you how fond we are of you and how much we admire your art." Dismayed, Cézanne stared at Monet: "You too are making fun of me." He turned, took his coat and left. (4, p. 188)

Hypersensitivity, suspicion, feelings of betrayal, and irascibility ran throughout Cézanne's emotional life. But even in the face of these internal demons, and perhaps intensified by them, his genius created a revolutionary and profoundly beautiful body of work that continues to command the stage of modern art.

REFERENCES

1) Rainer Maria Rilke: *Letters on Cézanne*. North Point Press, New York, 2002.

2) Maurice Merleau-Ponty: *Sense and Non-Sense*. Northwestern University Press, Chicago, 1964.

3) Russell, J: *The Meanings of Modern Art*. Harper and Row, New York, 1981.

4) Rewald, J: *Cézanne: A Biography*, Abrams, New York, 1986.

5) Dancher, A: *Cézanne, a Life*. Pantheon Books, New York, 2012.

PAUL GAUGUIN (1848–1903)

⌘

METAMORPHOSIS

Paul Gauguin's paintings are a central part of the post-Impressionist canon. He is recognized as a key figure in the creation of modernism, and his work influenced both Picasso and Matisse. Alongside Baudelaire and Mallarmé in poetry, and Debussy in music, Gauguin is a representative of the late 19th Century Symbolist movement, which rejected naturalism and realism and privileged spirituality, the imagination, mythology, and dream-states.

In the popular mind, Gauguin's life is the stuff of legend. In reality, as his biographer Andersen observed, "Few men worked harder at creating a self-image for others to see than Gauguin. As consciousness of his artistic potential grew he began to court his image wooing it with ardor until his life was given over to it." (1, p. 2) Tahiti, where he spent the latter part of his life, was for Gauguin a "lost paradise" despoiled by European colonization. Nonetheless, Polynesian mythology and the remnants of its original culture were the inspiration for much of his greatest achievements in art, which were "suffused with exotic light and color." (2, p. 9)

Of late, his work in media such as woodcut printing, ceramics, wood carving, monotype, and transfer drawing has garnered critical attention. (2, 3) Early 20th-century artists such as Edvard Munch were inspired by his woodcuts. The organizer of an exhibit of prints and transfer drawings at the Museum of Modern Art commented, "The transfer drawings represent Gauguin's final and perhaps most daring attempt to unify aspects of painting, drawing and print-making. And as the culminating invention of a decade of experimentation with various innovative print techniques they confirm that for Gauguin it was the creative process itself – the process of taking one thing and working to transform it into something radically new – that mattered above all else." (3, p. 32)

Gauguin was born in Paris, the younger of two children. His mother was of Peruvian descent, and his father was a journalist. Before Gauguin was born, his maternal grandmother traveled alone to Peru to petition – fruitlessly – for her portion of the family estate. Three years after their marriage, Gauguin's parents and their son traveled to Peru with the same intent. His father died on the voyage. Gauguin lived in Lima with his mother for the next 4 years. This childhood experience of an exotic, colorful, culturally diverse world undoubtedly had a powerful impact.

As a young man Gauguin pursued a successful career in Paris as a stockbroker. Without any formal training he had already begun to paint. At 25 he married a Danish woman, with whom he had five children. In 1882 the French stock market crashed, he lost his job, and his family moved to his wife's family home in Copenhagen. Unable to make a living, he left his family and went back to Paris to pursue a full-time career as an artist. He barely saw his wife and children again.

Early in his artistic career he exhibited with the Impressionists, but he rapidly dissociated himself from them. His paintings were admired by Vincent van Gogh, who invited him to share a studio in Provence. This received the encouragement and material support of Vincent's art dealer brother Theo, who may have thought Gauguin's presence might help stabilize his increasingly emotionally volatile brother. Three months into their time together, Vincent became floridly psychotic, threatened Gauguin's life, amputated his own ear, and was hospitalized. Gauguin fled back to Paris.

Stuckey observes that "the continuous spirit that guided Gauguin as an artist between 1880 and 1882 is reflected in his pioneering partisanship as a collector of works by Cézanne ... Cézanne would serve as the model for Gauguin the prophet in Tahiti, far removed from contemporary critical debate to meditate on ancient values and thus renew art at its source." (4, p. 13)

In 1891, Gauguin made his first voyage to Tahiti, where he remained until 1895. He had contemplated various other destinations such as Indo-China and Madagascar before settling on Tahiti. He wrote to the great Symbolist painter Odilon Redon (1840-1916): "I will go to Tahiti and I hope to finish out my life there." (4, p. 210) He envisioned a life of "ecstasy, calm and art" as he wrote to his wife Mette while simultaneously abandoning her and their children.

Gauguin wrote an account of his first sojourn in Tahiti entitled *Noa Noa* which means "fragrant" in Polynesian. Stuckey notes that "*Noa Noa* is a sensationalist account of Gauguin's bigamy with a Polynesian child bride" (4, p. 210) who became his model and informant concerning Tahitian culture which was incorporated into his remarkable paintings of this period. She also became pregnant.

In 1895, Gauguin returned to France to exhibit his Tahitian paintings which received mixed reviews and he returned to Tahiti where he remained for the last decade of his life.

Brettell observes that: "During the eight years that elapsed between Gaugin's final departure from France and his death on the distant island of Hivaoa in the Marquesas he was in the hospital at least four times often for prolonged periods; claimed to have attempted suicide once and perhaps succumbed to its temptations in 1903; built three houses; fathered at least three children; edited one newspaper and wrote, designed and printed another; completed three book length texts; sent paintings and drawings to many European exhibitions; finished nearly 100 paintings; made over 400 wood cuts; carved scores of pieces of wood; wrote nearly 150 letters. (4, p. 389)

During this period, two years after his return to Tahiti, destitute and depressed, he ascended into the mountain wilderness outside of Papeete and swallowed arsenic. He vomited the poison, staggered back to his studio, and proceeded to create one of his greatest paintings *D'où Venons-vous? Que somme-nous? Où allons-nous? (From where do we come? What are we? Where are we going?)* (now in the Boston Museum of Fine Arts). Gauguin now became involved in acrimonious disputes with the French colonial authorities and missionaries, whom he accused of corruption and insensitivity to the indigenous culture. He moved to a remote island in the Marquesas, hoping to find a "purer" Polynesia. By this time his health was deteriorating, and in 1903 he died of heart failure.

Gauguin prided himself on his transformation from "civilized European" to "savage savant." (2, p. 9) This paralleled his artistic journey, in which he practiced taking one technique and turning it into something radically different. Central to Gauguin's life is his quest for a lost paradise. One could speculate that the origins of this lay in a desire to recapture the lost paradise of his Peruvian childhood.

REFERENCES

1) Andersen, WV: *Gauguin's Paradise Lost*. New York, Viking Press, 1971.

2) Wright, A, Brown C: *Gauguin's Paradise Remembered: The Noa Noa Prints*. New Haven, Conn, Yale University Press, 2010.

3) Childs, E, Foster, H: *Gauguin Metamorphoses*. New York, Museum of Modern Art, 2014.

4) *The Art of Paul Gauguin*. Catalogue of an exhibition organized by the National Gallery of Art, Washington DC. Published by the New York Graphic Society, Little and Brown and Company, New York, 1988.

PROVOCATEURS

❧

GUSTAVE COURBET (1819-1877)
EGON SCHIELE (1890-1918)

The two artists described in this chapter both expressed through their art a desire to show raw sexuality thus stimulating – particularly in Schiele's case – social uproar and condemnation. Over time, the intrinsic beauty of their work, its basis in 'Realism', and its emotional power has become acknowledged. Both were radical and immensely talented artists, opposed to convention and authority.

Tillier quotes Courbet: "They call me the 'socialist painter'. I accept that title with pleasure. I am not only a socialist but a democrat and Republican as well – in a word – a partisan of all the revolution and above all a 'Realist'—for 'Realism' means a sincere lover of the honest truth." (1, p. 19)

Courbet's greatest claim to artistic fame is this embrace of 'Realism' expressed in his extraordinary paintings. 'Realism' became a driving force for many 19th and 20th Century artists.

Berger observed: "Because Courbet was uncompromising in his convictions, because his work and his way of life 'vulgarly' proved that art was as relevant to the back-parlor, the workshop, the cell as to the drawing room; because his paintings never offered the slightest possibility of escape from the world as it was, he was officially rejected in his lifetime and has since been only grudgingly admitted." (2, p. 226)

Further Berger observes: "A magnificent nude in front of a window and landscape is an uncompromising portrayal of a woman undressed – the picture evokes shock of the unexpected loneliness of nudity – the personal shock that inspires lovers, expressed in another way in Giorgone's *Tempest*."

Courbet was born in Ornans, a small town in the Franche Comte near the Swiss border. The countryside is characterized by limestone, deep valleys and streams and waterfalls. Berger observes: "I would guess that water occurs in some form or other, in about two-thirds of Courbet's paintings – Running water must have been one of the first sights and sounds that he experienced." (2, pp. 230-231)

Courbet was the eldest of four children and the only son in a relatively prosperous land-owning family. At the age of twenty-one, he came to Paris to become a painter, much against his father's will. By 1850, he had fashioned his 'Realist' style exemplified by his great painting *A Burial at Omans* (now in The Musee d'Orsay, Paris). A provincial funeral is treated with powerful realism on a heroic stage previously reserved for religious and historical subjects. This painting caused a sensation and Courbet continued to create provocative works such as *Le Sommeil* (now in The Musee des Beaux de la Ville de Paris) which portrayed two naked women entwined in bed.

His political activities during the time of the Paris Commune (1870) were to cause him considerable grief. He wrote a letter proposing that the column in the Place de Vendome erected by Napoleon to celebrate his martial victories be taken down stating: "the Vendome column is a monument devoid of all artistic value, tending to perpetuate by its expression the ideas of war and conquest of the past imperial dynasty, which are reproved by a republican nation's sentiment, citizen Courbet expresses the wish that the National Defense will authorize him to disassemble this column."

It was duly destroyed, but after the suppression of the Commune, Courbet was imprisoned and then told by the newly-installed right-wing government that he was to pay the cost of rebuilding the column. It was impossible for him to do so and he went into exile in Switzerland, financially ruined. His life had been devastated. He succumbed to alcoholism and died of liver disease aged 58.

Vienna at the end of the 19th Century was a creative epicenter that spawned radical artistic and intellectual innovation. As Schorske has noted: "Vienna in the *fin de siècle*, with its acutely felt tremors of social and political disintegration, proved one of the most fertile breeding grounds of the 20th Century's a-historical culture. Its great intellectual innovators – in music and philosophy, in economics and architecture and, of course, psycho analysis – all broke, more or less deliberately, their ties to the historical outlook central to the 19th Century liberal culture in which they had been reared." (3, p. xviii)

Egon Schiele was a product of this cultural ferment and alongside Gustav Klimt was one of the period's most important and original artists. Klimt, a central figure in the Viennese Secessionist movement, became famous and wealthy for his abstractly ornamented sensual portraits of Viennese society women. Klimt who was both professionally established and considerably older, recognized Schiele's talent and facilitated his gallery showings. Schiele, who was also a powerful portraitist and accomplished landscape painter, is best known for his watercolors and drawings with their graphic and unflinching display of the naked or, more often than not, half-clothed bodies and explicit display of genitalia. He made radical formal innovations and as Danto has suggested: "In Schiele's work the human body expresses its sexuality as artistic truth." (4) Classical concepts of beauty were jettisoned by Schiele as his self-portraits with their distortions of physiognomy demonstrate. A contemporaneous parallel to Schiele's and Klimt's expression of the primacy of sexuality can be found in Freud's creation of "libido" theory and his publication of the Dora case (1905) wherein a late adolescent in psychoanalytic treatment is subjected, not necessarily therapeutically, to one breath-taking sexual interpretation after another. Sex was certainly in the air of early 20th Century Vienna.

Schiele was a middle child with an older and younger sister. His father was the station-master of a provincial Austrian village who died of progressive syphilis when Schiele was 14. From being relatively comfortable, the family became impoverished and dependent on wealthier relatives. Schiele began drawing at an early age and, at his local school, found an important mentor who introduced him to Jugenstil, an Austro-German variant of art nouveau. Abandoning his father's early desire that he become a civil engineer, he obtained admission to the Vienna Academy of Fine Arts which had stringent admission standards. (Some years later this institution was to reject the application of the aspiring "artist" Adolph Hitler. The history of the 20th Century might have been quite different if he had been admitted). At age 16, Schiele was the youngest student admitted to his class. He came to hate the Academy with its rote antiquated curriculum and by 1909 left the school having already exhibited publically in Vienna alongside Klimt and developed the beginnings of his signature Expressionist style.

By 1910, Kallir observes: "Schiele resolved the conflict between decorative abstraction and conventional realism that had plagued Klimt's figural paintings by creating a new expressive pictorial language that leveled the formal and representational aspects of his compositions." (5)

In 1911, Schiele met the 17-year-old model Valerie Neuzel with whom he cohabited until his marriage to Edith Harms in 1915. In 1912 the police raided Schiele's studio in the village of Neulengbach and "erotic" works involving teenage models were found and seized. He was tried on the grounds of "public immorality" and sentenced to prison for three weeks. Nonetheless, his career flourished, he found wealthy patrons and created a series of searing self-portraits. In 1915 Schiele married and was inducted into the Austro-Hungarian army. He was assigned an office job in Vienna with considerable flexibility and brought his artistic productivity to new heights. In October 1918, his wife contacted Spanish influenza, a pandemic that would kill more people world-wide than the carnage of the First World War. Right before her death he sketched his moribund wife and two days later he succumbed to the same illness. He was 28.

Schiele's *œuvre* is complex and challenging to the viewer. He has been accused of "pornography" by some critics, yet Kallir probably captures the essence of his work best when she states: "Schiele is one of the only male artists ever to credit female sexuality with its true power, a power that academic convention through the ages has sought to deny and conceal." (5, p. 142)

Both Courbet and Schiele were artistic radicals who challenged conventional propriety. This was manifest not only in their art but in their personalities.

REFERENCES

1) Tillier, B: *Courbet: Utopia versus Politics In Catalogue of an Exhibition*, Gustave Courbet at The Metropolitan Museum of Art, New York, 2008.

2) Berger, J: *Portaits: John Berger on Artists*. Verso London and New York, 2015.

3) Shorske, CE: *Fin de siecle Vienna*.Vintage Books, New York, 1981.

4) Danton, AC: *Live Flesh*. *The Nation*. January 26, 2006 (online).

5) Kallir, J: *Egon Schiele: Drawings and Watercolors*. Thames & Hudson. London and New York, 2003.

JOSEPH CORNELL (1903–1972)

❧

THE HEART IS A LONELY HUNTER OF DREAMS

Surrealism arose in the 1920s in Paris, profoundly influenced by Freud's creation of psychoanalysis with its emphasis on the power of the dynamic unconscious in determining human behavior and its expression in dream states. The Frenchman André Breton, who had trained in medicine and psychiatry and who had engaged in the treatment of World War One veterans who were suffering from post-traumatic stress disorder, was the movement's progenitor.

Freud's technical concept of 'free association' in the psychoanalytic clinical situation became the surrealist credo for creative expression. Breton's 1924 Surrealist manifesto (1) extolled "psychic automatism" in creative work free of rational restraints and he extolled dream-states as the essence of creativity.

This credo was adapted by a number of innovative artists, including the Spanish film-maker Luis Buñuel (*cf. Un chien andalou*, a short film made with its graphic image of an eye-ball being sliced), the Spanish artist Joan Miró, as well as Max Ernst and René Magritte. The Italian painter de Chirico with his dream-like cityscapes was a precursor of Surrealism.

Surrealism had a significant impact on later artists such as Jackson Pollock and Mark Rothko in the early stages of their careers before they evolved into 'pure' abstract expressionists where they nevertheless maintained the Surrealist concept of 'spontaneity'.

Joseph Cornell was an heir to this tradition. As Waldman notes: "Cornell's art gives full expression to the many aspects of his personality. His principal contribution ... lies in the development of his 'shadow boxes', small-scale contributions in which painted papers, reproductions, sand, clay pipes and other found objects are assembled in a kind of collage with depth framed in wood and usually sealed with glass." (2, p. 13) Again, as Waldman observes: "Cornell had a tremendous influence ... his evocative arrangements of objects inspired Robert Rauschenberg's later collages and assemblages. Cornell's innovative use of film influenced artists such as Andy Warhol." (2, p. 13) Further, as Waldman asserts: "Cornell's deeply reverential attitude towards the universe as a mirror of mysterious truths is conveyed in each and every one of his box constructions." (2, p. 13)

Cornell was born in Nyack, New York, an attractive village perched above the Hudson river. His father was a successful designer and merchant of textiles. Cornell was the oldest of four children. His younger brother Robert suffered from severe cerebral palsy and was seriously disabled. Cornell was a major attendant of his brother in later life when Cornell, his mother and Robert moved to Utopia Parkway in Queens, New York. Cornell's father died when Joseph was 15, leaving the family in strained circumstances.

Through a well-connected family friend, Cornell was admitted to the prestigious Phillips Academy prep school but did not graduate. Cornell lived most of his life in a modest house in Queens with his somewhat tyrannical mother and disabled brother Robert. He never travelled beyond the immediate environs of New York City.

He received no formal training in art, briefly worked as a sales-man for a textile factory, was laid-off during the Depression and by age 37 had committed himself to his art. Beset by various gastro-intestinal ailments he embraced Christian Science. Waldman notes that: "Christian Science sustained him through a number of crises … Cornell found Christian Science just a few years before he encountered Surrealism. The confluence of these two beliefs, both of which dealt with the metaphysical nature of existence provided him with a life-long framework for his art." (2, p. 17)

Cornell pursued an active albeit solitary cultural life in New York, visiting museums, while simultaneously trolling second-hand bookstores and shops that specialized in bric-a-brac, collecting stamps, star-maps, clay pipes and wooden birds that would later become central to his shadow-boxes. By 1931, he began creating assemblages. By the early 1930s he received recognition from the larger art-world and was included in a landmark exhibition at the Museum of Modern Art in 1936.

Cornell greatly admired the transcendent French artist Chardin's *Soap Bubbles* (1734, now in the collection of the National Gallery of Art, Washington, DC) and subsequently wrote about its impact on his series of Soup Bubble sets." Shadow boxes become poetic theaters or settings wherein are metamorphosed the elements of a childhood pastime. The fragile, shimmering globules become the shimmering but more enduring planets – a connotation of moon and tides – the association of water, less subtle, as when drift-wood pieces make up a proscenium to set off the dazzling white of sea-foam and billowing cloud crystallized in a pipe of fantasy." (3)

In middle-life, Cornell was preoccupied with young ballerinas and created a number of boxes devoted to them and developed a number of platonic adoring relationships with some of the leading New York dancers of the 1950s. He was also entranced in his fantasy life by movie stars such as Marlene Dietrich, Marilyn Monroe, Jean Seberg and others. As Waldman observes: "Cornell's relationship to women was one of intensity and distance ... his most fulfilling artwork were dedicated to women about whom he could only dream." (1, p. 36)

Waldman describes Cornell, whom she knew personally, as: "a tall, thin man with a large head, graying hair, and hooded but piercing blue eyes ... his own remarks were hard to follow. He would digress from the most insignificant comment to the most meaningful one, following a train of thought that abruptly shifted gears, precise at one moment, obscure the next." (1, p. 6)

Even after he had achieved considerable fame, Cornell remained ensconced in his modest family home on Utopia Parkway, tending to his brother and his mother. His one important reality-based romantic relationship with the artist Yayoi Kusama (an important figure in the 1960s New York art world with her innovative creation of 'happenings' and other radical art) was vehemently opposed by his possessive mother. (4) Kusama commented in a recent film documentary of her life and work: "Joseph didn't like sex and nor did I so we really got along." (5) Kusama was twenty-six years younger and they were in daily contact and he made nude sketches of her. Their relationship continued even after her return to Japan and ended only when Cornell died in 1972 of probable heart-failure. His brother Robert and his mother had pre-deceased him.

Waldman eloquently summarized his artistic corpus: "In contrast to the Abstract Expressionists, whose work was expansive, Cornell's work was compressed. Each of his works made reference to an experience, a person, or a thing that had captivated him, whether it was a Medici prince, the night sky, a particular ballerina, or movie star, a hotel in France or a cockatoo." (1, p. 6) And further: "He saw, he dreamed, he imagined, and if a dream did not turn out as he wished and he was disillusioned ... then he would find other dreams and other paths to follow ... The boxes were his way of preserving his dreams." (1, p. 139)

Ultimately, what can be said about Cornell's unusual personality and reclusive genius? That he was, for the most part, socially isolated and lived a hermetic life peopled by his erotic fantasies of unattainable ballerinas and movie stars is apparent. Yet within this strange inner world be created works of great beauty that spoke to the fecundity of both his mind and the material world all encompassed and contained by his great shadow-boxes, with their essentially Surrealist technique of unexpected juxtapositions, which may be the best description of Cornell's psychology.

REFERENCES

1) Breton, A: *Manifest du Surrealism.* Editions du Sagittaire, Paris, 1924.

2) Waldman, D: *Joseph Cornell: Master of Dreams.* Harry N Abrams, New York, 2002.

3) Exhibition Catalogue: *Joseph Cornell Objects.* Copley Galleries, Beverly Hills, California, September 28, 1948.

4) Solomon, D: *Utopia Parkway: The Life and Work of Joseph Cornell,* Farrar, Straus and Giroux, New York, 1997.

5) Kusama: Infinity. A documentary directed by Heather Lenz, 2018.

6) Sheftel, S: *The Cosmic Child: The Artwork of Joseph Cornell and a Type of Unusual Sensibility or Thinking Inside the Box: The Mind that Channels Infinity.* The Psychoanalytic Study of the Child. Vol. 64 pp. 54-74. Yale University Press, New Haven and London, 2009.

AFTERWORD

❦

You do not have to be mad to be a great artist. You do, however, have to possess genius.

This does not, *ipso facto*, translate into mental illness.

Mental illness in great artists is no different from mental illness in the populace at large – it is ubiquitous. And just as mental illness filtered through the personality, psychology and character of any person so beset will have a profound effect on life-course, so it goes with the artist.

Nonetheless, the thesis of this book is that the complex and disparate mental disturbances of the great artists who are described here had a crucial influence on their creative achievements.

The French philosopher Maurice Merleau-Ponty (1908-1961) who introduced phenomenology to France wrote an insightful study called Cézanne's doubt (1). He said: "Thus the 'hereditary traits', the 'influences' – the accidents in Cézanne's life – are the text which nature and history gave him to decipher. They give only the literal meaning of his work. But an artist's creations, like a man's free decisions, impose on this given a figurative sense which did not pre-exist in them. If Cézanne's life seems to us to carry the seeds of his life within it, it is because we get to know his work first and see the circumstances of his life through it, changing them with a meaning borrowed from that work. If the givens for Cézanne which we have been enumerating, and which he spoke of as pressing conditions, were to figure in the web of projects which he was, they could have done so only by presenting themselves to him as what he had to live, leaving how to live it undetermined. An imposed theme at the start, they become, when replaced in the existence of which they are part, the monogram and the symbol of a life which fully interpreted itself. But let us make no mistake about this freedom. Let us not imagine an abstract force which could superimpose its effects on life's "givens" or which causes breaches in life's development. Although it is certain that a man's life does not explain his work, it is equally certain that the two are connected. The truth is that this work to be done called for this life." (1, p. 20)

The urge for creative expression is a distinguishing feature of humanity. In 1994, in the Ardeche valley of South-East France, the Chavet cave was discovered. Dating back some 30,000 years to the Paleolithic period, the cave-walls are covered with the earliest known paintings. Portrayals of animals of the time, they are remarkably sophisticated in their use of perspective and ability to convey dynamic motion. They speak to an intrinsic human artistic "drive", a desire to leave an imperishable that transcends mortality.

With regard to this creative "drive", Eugene Delacroix (1798-1863), the great French painter who was much admired by later artists as diverse as Renoir, Cézanne and Picasso asserted: "I have no love for reasonable painting. There is in me an old leaven, some black depth which must be appeased. If I am not quivering and excited like a serpent in the hands of a soothsayer, I am uninspired. I must recognize this and accept it. Everything good I have done has come to me this way." (2, p. xv)

The engagement with great art has the potential for changing the viewer. The British psychiatrist and pediatrician D.W. Winnicott

(1896-1971) wrote about the interplay between inner and outer reality, crystallized in his highly original concept of the "transitional object" which all infants embrace in their special blanket or stuffed toy, an object" that becomes self and other, and a creative world in between. (3) Transitional object can be extended to "transitional phenomena," wherein a psychological space is created between the art and viewer that involves both subject and object and is potentially original in its own regard. The "transference" that arises between clinician and patient' to which both creatively contribute is a further example of transitional phenomena specific to the psychotherapeutic situation.

One of the pleasures of writing this book is the immersion in the life and work of remarkable artists. After a while, as Pope-Hennessy reflected, they become "friends", albeit complex friends in their variety. It is a singular pleasure to have engaged with them and hence developed a "transitional" space.

REFERENCES

1) Merleau-Ponty, M: *Sense and Non-Sense*. (translators Dreyfus, HL & Dreyfus, PA). Northwestern University Press. www.nupress.northwestern.edu. 1964.

2) *The Journal of Eugene Delacroix*. Translated by Lucy Morton. Phaidon Press Inc. New York, 2010.

3) Winnicott, DW: *Transitional Objects and Transitional Phenomena*. International Journal of Psychoanalysis, Vol. 34, pp. 89-97, 1953.

www.ingramcontent.com/pod-product-compliance
Lightning Source LLC
Chambersburg PA
CBHW060245030426
42335CB00014B/1604